The Innovative Secretary

The Innovative Secretary

Marlene Caroselli, Ed.D.

SkillPath Publications
Mission, Kansas

Project Editor: Kelly Scanlon

Editor: Jane Doyle Guthrie

Book Design: Rod Hankins

Cover Design: Rod Hankins and Roger Ridpath

Library of Congress Catalog Card Number: 95-69804

ISBN: 1-878542-85-0

10   9   8   7   6   5   4   3   2   98   99   00

Printed in the United States of America

Contents

Introduction

Imagination takes vision out of its tunnel! And once freed from a confining space, vision can become an innovative reality. Imagination is not the private domain of the rare few who are able to see something new while others look at something old. Creative skills can be honed by anyone—despite the assertion of those self-doubting individuals who proclaim there's not a single creative bone in their bodies.

In this era of empowerment, secretaries in particular have opportunities as never before to contribute—to streamline processes, to eliminate waste, to form new partnerships. In these days of restructuring, reengineering, and reinventing, secretaries are discovering their own "re-" word: "redefining." The redefinition, however, begins with imagining what their roles could be like and then persuading others that the new definition has benefit for all concerned. *The Innovative Secretary* explores twenty-five traits that define the innovative secretary. Accompanying each trait are two exercises that will help you refine and develop the trait. The exercises are directly related to the secretarial realm: with secretaries taking on new responsibilities, new abilities are needed. Among the most valuable of these is the ability to innovate.

"Imagination," Tom Peters tells us, "is the only source of real value in the new economy." The secretarial role is changing and so is the perceived value of the role. As Einstein asserted, "Imagination is more important than knowledge." And today's secretaries need imaginative skills in order to apply the knowledge they already possess and to develop the knowledge they have yet to acquire.

We have become a service economy: 75 percent of us are in service industries rather than manufacturing firms. Peter Drucker, the father of modern management science, calls us "knowledge workers." As such, we depend more on mental, and less on manual, labor. And in these cyberspace conditions, we find words are the common currency. The poet Wallace Stevens has commented upon a powerful element in this new economy: "In the world of words, the imagination is one of the forces of nature."

In these pages, you will meet secretaries from Rio de Janeiro, Brazil, to Columbus, Ohio, who not only have articulated a vision but achieved it as well. Their stories will inspire you. Let their words stimulate your own imaginations. Become a force of nature yourself.

John Sculley asserts, "The best way to be ready for the future is to invent it." Secretaries who wish a better tomorrow for themselves and for their footstep-followers must be willing to invent the kind of future they wish to have.

Tolerates Ambiguity

Creative people tolerate ambiguity well, knowing that in time the ambiguous state will become better defined. They are comfortable when presented with the unknown. In fact, they often feel exhilarated as they contemplate a new problem. Complexity, opposing thoughts, vague outcomes—these do not daunt the creative individual who feels a heady excitement at the prospect of pushing existing boundaries.

Just as our ancestors became explorers and immigrants, creative people have the pioneering spirit that encourages moving beyond the known to the unknown, tearing down existing barriers in order to see new vistas.

One technique you can practice to bring you closer to an idealized state is to engage in fantasy. Fantasizing helps you to let go of the need for exactitude and to feel comfortable in situations that may not be well-defined. Don't underestimate the power of the imagination. Should you start to feel guilty for daydreaming, remember Einstein's words: "When I examined myself and my methods of thought, I came to the conclusion that the gift of fantasy has meant more to me than my talent for absorbing knowledge."

3

Exercise:

Tolerate ambiguity by fantasizing.

If you wish to increase your capacity for imagining, try engaging in fantasy from time to time. What would you imagine as a secretary's dream scenario? Record your thoughts after reading the samples provided.

> *"Good morning, Mr. X! Let me remind you that your first conference today will start within ten minutes. You'll meet our technical division people on the second floor. All the material you need for this presentation is on your table. After the conference, I'll give you the messages from last week. Would you like anything else before you leave?"*

What are your impressions of the secretary in this fantasy? Within six sentences, a distinct image has been created. Do you see a partnership at work, born of respect for and consideration of everyone's needs and talents? You may also have noticed a crisp efficiency operating as well.

The following fantasy, however, projects a different impression.

> *"Good morning, Ms. X! You're a few minutes late for our meeting but don't worry. I know how terrible traffic can be. Before we begin, would you mind getting me a cup of coffee. With cream …that's right. [Pause.] Thank you. Oh, you'll need your steno pad—I have quite a few points to make. To begin, we have to institute a 20 percent raise for me—effective immediately. Next, I have been thinking about your proposal to hire an assistant for me. I've come to the conclusion that you are correct—I am overworked. So, yes, let's proceed with that. Finally, I'd like to have some business cards made. Could you handle that for me? The title? 'Secretarial Executive' will be fine!"*

What would your secretarial fantasy be like? Be creative. You can't achieve something you cannot imagine. Record your thoughts here:

Good morning, Ms. X!

_____

_____

_____

_____

_____

_____

_____

_____

_____

_____

_____

Tolerates Ambiguity

Exercise:

Tolerate ambiguity by bridging existing and future states.

It's been said that nothing is as real as a dream. In the preceeding exercise, you fantasized a future state with conditions quite different from those you work in today. One way to bring your dreams closer to your realities is to bridge existing and future states. In other words, what would it take to have tomorrow's dream supplant today's reality?

Yes, the future is uncertain. Ambiguity surrounds the present. It is true that no one really knows what's in store for our world, our country, our organization, ourselves. And yet, we all have the capacity to influence the future, to shape the circumstances that could easily become reality. That's what vision is all about.

There was a time, for instance, when there were no professional organizations for secretaries. There was a time when the Certified Professional Secretaries (CPS) degree did not exist. There was a time when the United States did not honor secretaries in April. But all these became realities because someone had a dream. Imaginative people can tolerate ambiguity. They have faith in their ability to carve distinct shapes from the amorphous mass known as "tomorrow."

A. List here your current job conditions. (If you prefer, you could list realities that exist for secretaries in general.)

_____

_____

_____

_____

_____

_____

B. Now explain what the ideal job would be like. (Or, in more global terms, explain what could be considered the ideal state for all secretaries.)

_____

_____

_____

_____

_____

_____

C. Finally, describe what it would take to create that future state. What plans must you implement? What "bridges" would you have to build in order to move from the reality of the present to the "ideality" of the future?

_____

_____

_____

_____

_____

_____

Is Willing to Explore

The innovative secretary is willing to explore new ideas, to examine new possibilities, to allow the "known" to forge a path for the "unknown." Of course, it's more secure to remain with the existing circumstances, but if our ancestors had not been willing to explore, most of us would not be here today. While it can be uncomfortable to leave the familiar behind, it can also be a rousing experience. A sense of adventure permeates the lives of those who view uncharted territory with eagerness.

Exercise:

Explore possibilities with a new word.

The word *secretary* has undergone significant change since the profession was born in ancient Rome. There, the secretary (derived from the word "secretarius") was a person who could be trusted with secrets. Today, of course, the secretary is still the trusted confidante, but the job includes responsibilities that go far beyond the original sphere of influence.

For years, secretaries have questioned the appropriateness of the term that describes their function. Alternatives, of course, have been suggested: "administrative assistant," "office administrator," "support staff specialist."

For this exercise, try to come up with a brand-new word or phrase—one that no one has ever used before. One that's not in the dictionary. One that captures the true essence of what secretaries do. Just as the word "avionics" was created to depict the impact of electronics on aviation, and just as Coach Pat Riley created the word "threepeat" to describe the success of a team that wins three basketball championships in a row, so can you create a word that no one else has heard—yet.

Here are some neologisms (newly created words) to get you started:

multitary   to reflect having more than one boss

cybertary   to reflect increased computer responsibilities

paramanager   to reflect tasks increasingly managerial in nature

datalyst   to reflect work that needs a head and not just hands

What neologisms can you devise? _____

_____

_____

_____

_____

_____

_____

_____

_____

Exercise:

Use "what if" thinking to explore new avenues of thought.

When you engage in "what if" thinking, you force your mind to travel new pathways. This process is the stuff of which innovation is born. Consider this hypothetical situation: "What if God had had a secretary?"

Some possible consequences of that subjunctive state are these:

The world would have been created in five days!

Secretaries would be regarded as earth angels.

Della Street and not Saint Peter would be guarding the gates of Heaven.

The word *secretary* would carry as much significance as the term *Secretary of State*.

No one would precede "secretary" with the words "just a."

Now respond to the following "what if" scenario: *What if secretaries were paid what they are worth?*

1. "Organizations would go broke" was probably your first thought. Continue thinking ... along more serious lines, if you can. Record your thoughts here: _____

   _____

   _____

   _____

   _____

   _____

   _____

   _____

2. Now specify one thing that you could do to make the possibility you suggested above a reality:_____

   _____

   _____

   _____

   _____

   _____

   _____

   _____

Is Receptive to New Ideas

Imaginative individuals keep their minds open—and, as a result, all kinds of ideas can fly in. In fact, it is staying receptive to new possibilities that helps them come up with new ideas. Experts tell us we should spend about one-third of our reading time perusing fields other than those we naturally gravitate to.

Innovative secretaries know that just because they've never heard of a person or a concept doesn't mean it doesn't exist or that it lacks value. And because they accept novelty, because they are willing to consider rather than to condemn, they not only welcome new ideas, they often create them!

Exercise:

Engage in "Janusian" thinking.

Janus was the ancient Roman god of the new year (hence, "January"). On coins, his face was shown looking in two directions: back over the recently passed year and forward to the new year. When you allow yourself to think in Janusian terms, you are able to look at any idea from two opposing points of view.

W. E. McMullan notes that "creative individuals are paradoxical personages." And Carl Jung has observed that "every creative person is a duality or a synthesis of contradictory aptitudes."

This exercise may bring new insights to both you and your manager. Begin by listing the things for which the typical boss is responsible for in a given week; in the next column, list the things the typical secretary is responsible for in a given week:

Boss	Secretary
_____	_____
_____	_____
_____	_____
_____	_____
_____	_____
_____	_____
_____	_____
_____	_____
_____	_____
_____	_____

Now go back and write an "S" beside those managerial functions you feel you could handle, in part or in full. Then place an "M" beside secretarial functions that a boss can, does, or should handle. (For example, typing, proofreading, and editing have long been functions of the secretary. Many a manager, however, now performs those functions—thanks to the advent of the computer.)

How could you persuade your boss to let you handle more managerial tasks? _____

_____

_____

_____

_____

_____

Exercise:

Be receptive to kinesthetic thoughts.

You can foster creativity when you consider a particular essence not in its usual sensory terms but rather in unusual sensory terms. This crossing of sensory inputs is known as "kinesthesia." For example, many people typically think of problems as situations that can be improved with thoughtful actions. But what if you consider problems as things you can see or touch or hear? For example, what if problems were water? Here are some kinesthetic responses to that very question from support staff personnel at Johnson Controls.

"If problems were water, I'd probably be swimming every day, but at the end, I'd make sure to grab a big towel and dry off." *Jenni Mastrogiovanni*

"If problems were water, I'd be drowning because I'm in way over my head. (The plus side is that—with a pack of Kool-Aid and some sugar—I'd never be thirsty.)" *CaSandra Mathis*

"If problems were water, I would float to the top." *Luonne Dumak*

"If problems were water, there would be a rain storm in my office daily." *Kathy Halbrooks*

"If problems were water, my cup runneth over." *Murphy Nieskes*

"If problems were water, I'd use them to feed my plants." *Brigid McGeehan*

"If problems were water, a sponge could absorb them all." *Dawn Tietyen*

Now it's your turn. Just relax and allow your mind to travel along some new paths. Think about this kinesthetic possibility:

If you could see stress, it would look like _____

_____

or _____

_____

or _____

_____

or _____

_____

or _____

_____

or _____

_____

or _____

_____

Now try a kinesthetic possibility of your own: _____

_____

_____

_____

Sees What Isn't There

A popular creativity spur is to look at what everyone else is looking at but to see what no one else is seeing. This, perhaps, is the very essence of creativity: doing the uncommon with the common, turning the familiar into the unfamiliar. We are surrounded with "reusabilities"—items that can either contribute to America's growing garbage problem or that can be put to new use. Secretaries who can salvage the throwaways and use them to save time, money, and the environment are the secretaries whose thinking skills are valued. Likewise, secretaries who practice looking at things and situations in uncommon ways will hone their ability to think creatively and suggest new ideas—from ways to save time on projects to streamlining office procedures.

Exercise:

Create new uses for old things.

Assume it's the day after Professional Secretaries Day and every secretary in your organization has a vase of wilting flowers. You hate to see them headed for the wastebasket, so you decide to spearhead a drive to rescue all those flowers and do something practical with them.

Record here what you can do beyond the obvious first two. Return to the page often if you don't finish it today. Ask for suggestions from other people and then... try implementing the best ideas next April!

1. Press them and make greeting cards with them.

2. Dry them for potpourri.

3. _____

4. _____

5. _____

6. _____

7. _____

8. _____

9. _____

10. _____

11. _____

12. _____

13. _____

14. _____
15. _____
16. _____
17. _____
18. _____
19. _____
20. _____
21. _____
22. _____
23. _____
24. _____
25. _____

Exercise:

Develop turnaround thinking.

"Turnaround thinking" will lead you to novel ideas—those untouched by triteness. All you need to do is take a familiar phrase or ordinary saying and turn it around so it becomes a wondrously new concept—untainted by hackneyed thought. A good example is Reverend Jesse Jackson's proclamation: "I was born in the slums but the slums were not born in me!" Or President Jimmy Carter's definition of America's genesis: "America did not invent human rights. Human rights invented America."

Here is a less serious turnaround: "Time heals all wounds" and its barbed counterpart, "Time wounds all heels." And an even less serious one: "I used to be lost in the shuffle. Now I just shuffle with the lost." Finally, delight in this from a frustrated but unknown member of Congress: "You can bring a House to order, but you can't make it think."

Think about the secretarial function and give it a fresh twist by turning around one (or more) of these common phrases:

add insult to injury	benefit of the doubt
all in a day's work	better late than never
all things being equal	bite off more than you can chew
as luck would have it	bite the bullet
ax to grind	bring home the bacon
bark up the wrong tree	can't see the forest for the trees
beat around the bush	cool as a cucumber
bend over backward	diamond in the rough

down in the dumps

easier said than done

face the music

fate worse than death

feather in your cap

feeling your oats

flash in the pan

get a foot in the door

handwriting on the wall

hard row to hoe

hit the nail on the head

hook, line, and sinker

in the final analysis

in the nick of time

irons in the fire

knock on wood

_____

_____

_____

_____

_____

_____

_____

_____

_____

_____

_____

_____

_____

_____

Regards Problems as Opportunities

The founder of L. L. Bean loved to hunt, but he hated coming home with wet leather boots. He used his discomfort to lead him to a solution—putting leather tops on rubber bottoms. Discomfort, albeit emotional rather than physical, was also the genesis of another innovative endeavor. Edwin Land had taken his family to Santa Fe for vacation. His five-year-old daughter asked him to take her photograph, which he did, happily. She *then* asked, "Daddy, can I see it?" It was difficult for Land to deny his daughter, but her question prompted him to think: "Perhaps I could invent a camera that would develop the film itself and produce a complete photograph within minutes." Thus, the Polaroid Land Camera was born.

Success is often a function of receptivity. The average person accepts today's reality as tomorrow's reality too. The innovator, by contrast, seeks to alter today's reality, to fulfill its promise for the future. Don't permit negatives to destroy possibilities. *Regard problems as opportunities.*

From time to time, think about Paul Schoemaker, an associate professor at the University of Chicago. He contends that all decisions are influenced by the way they're phrased when they're presented. As an experiment, he presented a plan to his students and asked for their input. He told half the students that the plan had an 80 percent chance of succeeding. The other half were told the plan had a 20 percent chance of failing. This, of course, is the same statistic—just presented from two different perspectives. However, the students who heard the word *success*, by a large majority, voted to proceed with the plan. The majority of those who heard the word *failure* voted to have him abandon the plan.

"Attitude," as they say, "is all."

Exercise:

Develop faith that opportunities exist in problems.

The energy for creativity is born in problems—problems that push us to change the status quo and move toward a better way. If necessity is the mother of invention, challenge is the father of creativity. Each day we face an onslaught of difficulties; occasionally they overwhelm us and we fall on our faces. But we have the capacity to rise again and again to tackle the obstacles that stand in our way. That is what life is all about.

The most resilient among us have found ways to meet challenges and sometimes even to profit from them. This exercise is designed to deepen your awareness of the silver linings that await just inside most "clouds."

Think about your life over the last five or ten years and list the most serious problems you can recall from that time span:

1. _____

2. _____

3. _____

4. _____

5. _____

6. _____

 _____

7. _____

 _____

8. _____

 _____

9. _____

 _____

10. _____

 _____

11. _____

 _____

12. _____

 _____

13. _____

 _____

14. _____

 _____

15. _____

 _____

Now go back and write an "O" beside each problem that had some positive result—some way in which you grew or were able to help others or became a stronger person or learned something beneficial. How many of those original problems were actually opportunities in disguise?

Exercise:

Look at problems from a new perspective.

One problem-solving technique that sometimes leads to innovative results is the "3F approach": Flaws, Failures, and Faults. Begin by briefly describing a problem you're currently facing: _____

_____

_____

_____

_____

Quickly list some solutions for this problem:_____

_____

_____

_____

_____

_____

Now choose the best of the above solutions and think of it in terms of the "3Fs."

Flaws
Imagine that your most severe critic were to find flaws in this solution. What flaws would that person cite? _____

_____

_____

_____

_____

As you review the flaws you expect a critic to point out, isolate one that might be legitimate. Use it to stimulate some action you might have forgotten to take, and specify that action here: _____

_____

_____

_____

Failure

How could this solution backfire? What might go wrong? What would happen if you tried to implement this solution and you failed miserably? List all the negative consequences you can think of:

_____

_____

_____

_____

If your decision/solution does fail, what is one positive result that you would realize? _____

_____

Faults

If the solution you are proposing were implemented and if the effects were damaging—disastrous even—who or what would be considered "at fault"? _____

_____

How could that blame be minimized or lessened? What precautions could be taken to soften the blow of accusations, even if the solution did not work as planned? _____

_____

_____

Assume all fingers were pointing at you as the person responsible for this poor decision. What benefits could you derive from an experience such as this?_____

_____

With the 3F method, you can learn to minimize mistakes by looking at your pending decision as a *fait accompli*. Even with careful, creative forethought, though, mistakes will occur. Whether or not you can then put a "positive spin" on these mistakes will depend on your attitude. Let these words of wisdom help you form that attitude:

"Stumbling is not falling."

Portuguese proverb

"He who has never made a mistake is one who never does anything."

Theodore Roosevelt

"If I wasn't making mistakes, I wasn't making decisions."

Robert W. Johnson

INTERVIEW: Heloiza Uzeda, Executive Secretary, Coca-Cola Industrias Ltda, Rio de Janeiro, Brazil

Q: *What inspires you to be creative?*

A: I like new things, new ideas, new situations at home, in the office, anywhere. That is the reason I am always looking for something to be modified or created.

Q: *What workplace examples of creativity (or creative solutions to problems) can you share?*

A: These examples are not particularly special, but they make the days easier, more efficient, or even more pleasant.

1. I created a new header for the memos we send from the Technical Department so that our memos could be recognized immediately when they were received.

2. Different subjects in my file are distinguished by different colors. It makes the search easier.

3. My boss gave me some photos to be sent to some bottlers. Instead of simply preparing a cover letter, I created a beautiful cover for them and also a frame. My boss complimented me on this "very good idea."

4. We have a staff meeting for our department each month. As it takes the whole afternoon, I always make arrangements for a break and I look for different kinds of food to be served for each meeting. Nowadays the break is so famous that my boss said the participants are as much interested in knowing what will be served at break as they are in knowing the subject of the meeting.

Q: *Your boss has many talents. Is creativity one of them? If so, how has he developed creativity? What does he do to encourage others to be creative?*

A: My boss is a creative person—he also admires creative ideas. He just says what he needs and asks us to develop the idea in the best way we can. He is always giving us challenges that, I believe, stimulate us to be creative.

Q: *How receptive is your boss to your creative ideas? How can you strengthen your partnership with your boss so he will be even more receptive to your ideas?*

A: He likes my ideas quite a bit. The most important thing, in my opinion, is to discover exactly what he expects me to do or what he desires for a particular task. It is also necessary to collect as many details as possible in order to meet his needs.

Q: *How does your organization encourage creativity in employees?*

A: The organization does not have any formal policy. However, there are many managers who stimulate their employees by encouraging them to attend specific courses, by delegating tasks, by continually asking employees for solutions.

Q: *Apply your creative thinking to this question, please: "What can secretaries around the world do to help one another?"*

A: Secretaries around the world can *exchange information.* That will be the most useful thing for our profession. We need to know what is happening in other companies in the same city, in other states, and also in other countries. We can evaluate the applicability of various ideas to our daily work. For this purpose, a center must be created to centralize the information received from secretaries all over the world. These secretaries should be listed on a formal list. The information received should be summarized in a report and then distributed to all the secretaries listed.

Is
Self-Directed

nnovative employees are inner-directed; they are entrepreneurial in spirit. They'd prefer to be given a general direction rather than detailed directions. Innovative secretaries like having trust placed in them, for trust means faith in their judgment and in their capability. There are attendant risks, of course: When someone else makes all the decisions, that person derives both the glory of success and the responsibility for failure. When you make the decisions, you derive the glory and the responsibility.

Human beings, like ships, are safe if they never leave the harbor. But also like ships, people weren't created to stay in harbors.

Exercise:

Test your S-D (self-direction) quotient.

A. Place an "X" in the column that indicates how each statement applies to you.

	Not at all	Somewhat	Absolutely
1. I like saying, "I did it my way."	☐	☐	☐
2. I'm known as a self-starter.	☐	☐	☐
3. I prefer direction to directions.	☐	☐	☐
4. I am a careful risk-taker.	☐	☐	☐
5. Achievement is important to me.	☐	☐	☐
6. I like having responsibility.	☐	☐	☐
7. I often take the initiative to get things started.	☐	☐	☐
8. I like being in charge.	☐	☐	☐
9. I cherish personal freedom.	☐	☐	☐
10. I am highly motivated.	☐	☐	☐
11. I am flexible and open-minded.	☐	☐	☐
12. I welcome feedback on my performance.	☐	☐	☐
13. I often assume the leadership role.	☐	☐	☐
14. I have a high energy level.	☐	☐	☐

B. Which of these scenarios comes closest to your interpretation of this picture?

1. This woman has finished organizing the retirement party for a co-worker. All the committees she set up have done what they had to do (except the cleanup committee). The final and most pleasant task was to purchase a gift with the moneys she collected. In a few hours, the fun will begin.

2. This woman understands the importance of occasional self-indulgence. She'd promised herself that once she'd completed a long and tedious project, she would reward herself. She completed the project on time and under budget, and she's rewarded herself for this outstanding accomplishment.

3. This woman likes nothing better than socializing. She's always being invited to get-togethers and, it seems, is always having them herself. On this occasion, with her "hostess gift" in hand, she's on her way to a friend's house for a holiday gathering.

Interpreting your responses:

In section A, how many "not at all" answers did you have? _____

If you had seven or more, you're probably more comfortable being directed by others than directing yourself. Certainly, there's nothing wrong with this preference. However, it will be difficult to become a creative achiever if you are unwilling to initiate things. If you had seven or more and if you really would like to become a creative achiever, tackle small undertakings, get feedback, and move on to more challenging tasks.

How many "somewhat" answers did you have? If you had seven or more, you have a solid foundation for innovation. People need to overcome psychological barriers before they can give their imaginations free reign. Seven or more "somewhats" indicate a willingness on your part to accept challenges. Many of those challenges will be ones you have established for yourself.

How many "absolutely" answers did you have? If you had seven or more, you are allowing your imagination to lead the way to new ventures and adventures. Channel that intellectual energy and focus it on situations in your office environment that need improvement.

For section B, answers 1 and 2 both indicate considerable self-direction.

Answer 3 indicates a strong interest in "affiliation" or being with other people. These assessments are based on work done over the past forty years by Harvard professor David McClelland, who uses pictures (Thematic Apperception Tests or TAT's) as a prompt to story telling. On the basis of the interpretations people make of the pictures they see, he has determined that people are driven by the need for achievement, the need to take charge, and/or the need to work with other people. There is no "right" or "wrong" need, but it's important to align these motivational needs or drives to the work you have elected to do.

Exercise:

Imagine directing yourself—and then work to create the reality.

"Intrapreneur" is a term Gifford Pinchot coined to describe the person who works as an entrepreneur inside an organization instead of taking his or her talents outside the organization to establish a business. When organizations make accommodations for intrapreneuring, everyone wins. The employee is given a degree of autonomy, of empowerment. For some people, this is a sine qua non as far as work is concerned. The organization profits too by retaining this talent and maximizing its potential.

But such situations do not merely happen. They begin as an idea that is carefully nurtured to fruition. Conceptualize being in charge of the office by imagining a single day during which you must direct the flow of work. Assume your boss was sent on an overseas assignment and you are left in charge of the office. Now imagine a typical day without him or her, and think about how the hours would be spent. Use the next page to list and describe those activities.

If I Were the Boss...

8:00 _____

8:30 _____

9:00 _____

9:30 _____

10:00 _____

10:30 _____

11:00 _____

11:30 _____

12:00 _____

12:30 _____

1:00 _____

1:30 _____

2:00 _____

2:30 _____

3:00 _____

3:30 _____

4:00 _____

4:30 _____

5:00 _____

Next, make a list of the phone calls you would likely receive in a typical day:

1. _____ Concerning _____

2. _____ Concerning _____

3. _____ Concerning _____

4. _____ Concerning _____

5. _____ Concerning _____

6. _____ Concerning _____

7. _____ Concerning _____

8. _____ Concerning _____

9. _____ Concerning _____

10. _____ Concerning _____

Look over the list now and place an "M" in front of the calls you could handle yourself. (Research shows that competent secretaries can handle 90 percent of the calls coming in to their offices.)

Think next about the written information that comes into your office each day—letters, memos, e-mail, faxes, reports, and so on. Jot down the typical day's worth of data:

1. _____

2. _____

3. _____

4. _____

5. _____

6. _____

7. _____

8. _____

9. _____

10. _____

Remembering that overseas communications can be expensive, which of the above would you need to send to your boss (place a "B" in front of the item number) and which could you handle yourself (place an "M" in front of those numbers)?

Finally, think about what it would take to convince your boss that you're capable of handling more responsibilities and fewer directions.

Is Able to Defer Judgment

The business world abounds with verbal murderers—those who can kill a good idea by uttering a few disparaging words. Some of those ideas are so brutally destroyed there is no hope of ever resuscitating them. Don't engage in "ideacide" yourself. Before you reject a thought as too expensive, too risky, or too complicated, engage in positive scrutiny. Allow the idea to incubate. In its altered, refined form, it may be totally workable. But if you inhibit ideas in their infancy, you'll never know their potential, and you'll have no way of gauging how serious the loss is. As W. Edwards Deming has noted, "The greatest losses are unknown and unknowable."

In some teams, members are free to "shoot down" the ideas of others. But before they utter their rejecting statements, they must offer three affirming statements. They must give three advantages of the idea, three ways in which it *could work.* Try this technique at your next team meeting, whenever the team is ready to discard a possibly beneficial proposal: acknowledge three strong points the idea has, re-think it, and *then* reject it if necessary. In addition to encouraging people to offer suggestions, the ideas themselves can be explored thoroughly instead of being rejected after only a superficial examination.

Exercise:

Engage in "gray" thinking.

"For every complex problem," H.L. Mencken commented, "there is one solution that is simple, neat, and wrong." All too often, we seek black-and-white answers when we should be looking for answers with multiple shades of gray. As individuals, as teams, as organizations, we succumb to the pressures of time and jump to quick solutions when in-depth analysis may be called for instead.

To help you go beyond the obvious, take a look at these two words: "red" and "brown".

What do they have in common?_____

_____

You probably noted that both were colors. Did you also note that:

- Both begin with a consonant?

- Both end with a consonant?

- Both have a single vowel in the middle?

- Both have another word inside ("Ed" and "own")?

- Both contain the letter "r"?

Get some practice in going beyond the obvious black-and-white answers by writing down the commonalties these words share.

1. Cadillac, Chevrolet, Camaro _____

_____

_____

_____

_____

2. lemon, apple, lime _____

_____

_____

_____

_____

3. Lincoln, Jefferson, Washington _____

_____

_____

_____

_____

4. gazelle, rabbit, squirrel _____

_____

_____

_____

_____

5. nightmare, daydream, woolgathering _____

_____

_____

_____

_____

Exercise:

Ignore the "mostbusters."

There are those who—deliberately or inadvertently—will dismiss or deny the potential you have for effecting positive change. These people are "mostbusters" for they "bust" your desire to "be the most you can be." The reasons why such individuals attempt to stifle innovation are numerous, but many can be related to Max DePree's wise observation: "The creative process in today's corporation is by its very nature difficult to handle. Anything truly creative results in change, and if there is one thing a well-run bureaucracy or institution or major corporation finds difficult to handle, it is change."

When you experience rejection, when others try to "bust" your innovative efforts, remember that what you're experiencing has been experienced by countless others who had good ideas. ("Every great oak," it has been observed, "was once a nut that stood its ground.") For this perseverance-promoting exercise, match the individuals on the left with the comments others have made about them.

1. Louis Pasteur

   A. Had first manuscript rejected by sixteen literary agents and twenty-four publishing houses

2. Guiseppe Verdi

   B. Was expelled from school after the principal said, "Your mere presence offends me"

3. Walt Disney

   C. Was declared "insufficiently talented"

4. Wilma Glodean Rudolph

   D. Was deemed a "mediocre" student

5. Winston Churchill

   E. Was called a "hopeless" alcoholic

6. Grandma Moses

   F. Was regarded as "insane" for trying to turn rubber into practical use

7. Thomas Edison

   G. Was considered too old to succeed

8. Albert Einstein

   H. Was labeled "too stupid to learn"

9. Charles Goodyear

   I. Was told he had no talent

10. Bill Wilson

   J. Was termed "dull" and failed sixth grade

11. John Grisham

   K. Was told she would never be able to walk normally

Answers: 1-D; 2-C; 3-I; 4-K; 5-J; 6-G; 7-H; 8-B; 9-F; 10-E; 11-A

Is Able to Concentrate

We live in chaotic times and often work in hectic environments. Each day, each hour, each minute, we are bombarded with a great variety of stimuli. In fact, scientists tell us we can process eight hundred ideas, words, images, impressions *a minute!* All of this makes staying focused a real challenge. A great many forces intrude on concentration, and a great many sensory inputs demand our attention—which is limited at best.

The good news, though, is that you can develop strong concentration skills. With the goal clearly defined and your mental faculties attuned to that goal, you can remain centered as you attempt to accomplish whatever the job requires.

Exercise:

Practice concentration.

One technique that will sharpen your ability to think only about one thing at a time is a practice exercise that resembles dialing a phone. For this exercise, you will need a page of telephone numbers as well as a timer.

Assume the numbers below are the buttons of a telephone. Set your timer for two minutes.

Place a mark at the top of one column from a page of phone-book numbers and begin to dial the numbers listed. When the timer goes off, place a mark next to the last number you dialed. Practice this skill-builder whenever you have two spare minutes. See how much beyond your first effort you can go. Date each effort so you can track your progress.

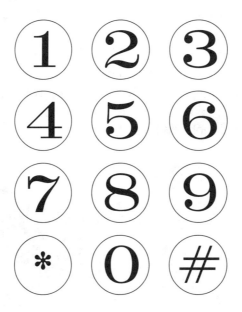

Exercise:

Set self-challenges.

Thomas Edison set self-challenges and then worked to fulfill his own prophecies. He decided upon the number of inventions he wanted to present to the Patent Office each week. In other words, he wooed his creative abilities instead of wailing that he had none. Here is a practice exercise that will not only increase your capacity for concentration, it should also inspire you to do better with each subsequent practice.

You will need a timer for this activity, which is done in this way. Look at these letters:

[dc]   [oa]   [gt]

If you look only at the letters on the left side of each bracketed item, they will spell the word "dog." And if you look only at the letters on the right side of each bracketed item, they will spell the word "cat." Set your timer now and see how long it takes you to determine the two words (one with letters on the left side of the bracketed pair and the other with letters on the right side of each bracketed pair) contained in each line. Record your starting time here: _____

1. [m c] [o o] [d m] [e e] [r d] [a i] [t a] [e n] _____

2. [m m] [a o] [t v] [e e] [r m] [i e] [a n] [l t] _____

3. [e a] [x r] [e r] [r o] [c g] [i a] [s n] [e t] _____

4. [p d] [r i] [o s] [f t] [o r] [u i] [n c] [d t] _____

5. [c c] [o o] [m n] [m t] [e i] [r n] [c u] [e e] _____

6. [q p] [u r] [e a] [s c] [t t] [i i] [o c] [n e] _____

Completion time: _____

How well did you do? Now that you have the hang of it, make a prediction for how long it will take you to do the next exercise. Can you better your first score? How long do you think it will take you to do the second exercise? Now record your starting time, set your timer, and get started.

Starting time: _____

  1. [i n] [d e] [e w] [n c] [t o] [i m] [f e] [y r] _____

  2. [a p] [d r] [e e] [q v] [u i] [a o] [t u] [e s]_____

  3. [c s] [o t] [m a] [p n] [u d] [t a] [e r] [r d] _____

  4. [e f] [m a] [p m] [l i] [o l] [y i] [e a] [r r] _____

  5. [r o] [e u] [g t] [i l] [o y] [n i] [a n] [l g] _____

  6. [v m] [i e] [o t] [l a] [e p] [n h] [c o] [e r] _____

Completion time: _____

By the way, you can work with a friend who is also interested in self-challenging activities. Each of you should make five or ten of the exercises and then exchange them with each other. To prepare the exercises, just find words with the same number of letters and write the words side by side, letter by letter, as shown in the exercise.

If you really like challenges, choose words longer than eight letters and make exercises that have more than six entries.

Is a Divergent Thinker

Oliver Wendell Holmes observed, "Man's mind stretched to a new idea never goes back to its original dimension." Here's a simple example of a mind-stretcher for you, designed to heighten your awareness of the need for divergent thinking.

Look at the following diagram and decide which letter doesn't belong and why:

b	c
d	g

Very often, as we work to solve problems or create new initiatives, we fail to use all the resources available to us. Why is this so? Sometimes we are so blinded by familiar ways of looking at things that we don't see what is right in front of our eyes. And so we neglect possibilities that could make us more efficient. Oh, yes. The correct answer. It's the letter "t." Why? Because the "t" in the diagram is bigger than the other four letters and also because it is not written as a shadow outline and the other four are. If you are like most people, though, you did not even see a "t" in the diagram.

Exercise:

Define your thinking style.

We all know a great deal, especially about ourselves. We know what we like—in art, in music, in food, in a friend. We know (are aware of) what we know about our jobs, our capacity to hold those jobs, and what it will take to continue being successful. But many of us don't know what our thinking style is.

Basically, we have one of two orientations—we depend either on the left hemisphere of the brain extensively or on the right. Neither one is good or bad, right or wrong. It's natural and normal to have such a dependency, just as it's accepted without question that some people are right-handed and others are left-handed.

The problem arises when we have to solve a problem that requires the characteristics of the *other* half of the brain, the one we don't usually use. Is it possible to develop the capacity of the nondominant sphere? Absolutely! In fact, the ideal is to become "lateralized"—able to switch to either sphere depending on the parameters of the problem.

Before you can begin to develop your seldom-used side, however, you need to determine which side you're currently using. Here are some true-or-false questions to help you decide that:

____ 1. I often depend on my intuition.

____ 2. I have a good vocabulary and good language skills.

____ 3. I have an efficient filing system.

____ 4. I make connections (see relationships) fairly easily.

____ 5. I have a good sense of humor and/or am known as a funny person.

____ 6. I consider myself (and/or am considered by others) as an emotional person.

_____ 7. I often decide to do things spontaneously.

_____ 8. I have always been good with numbers.

_____ 9. I prefer to read the owner's manual rather than experiment with a new purchase.

_____ 10. I daydream at least once a day.

_____ 11. I prefer the "bird's eye" view to the "worm's eye" view.

_____ 12. I am detail oriented.

_____ 13. I like to have all the facts before I make a decision.

Use the following chart to help you tally your choices. Circle the letter "R" or the letter "L" for each item, depending on the answer (true or false) you gave:

	True	False
1.	R	L
2.	L	R
3.	L	R
4.	L	R
5.	R	L
6.	R	L
7.	R	L
8.	L	R
9.	L	R
10.	R	L
11.	R	L
12.	L	R
13.	L	R

- How many "R" answers did you have? _____

- How many "L" answers? _____

If you had approximately the same number for each (a 6/7 combination, for example), you are probably lateralized, which is the ideal orientation. It suggests you are mentally "ambidextrous," capable of using either half of your brain, depending on the nature of the problem to be solved.

A majority of "R" answers indicates a right-brain orientation. You tend to be creative, imaginative, spontaneous. Your problem-solving style depends more on fantasy than on facts. To increase your left-brain skills, develop your organizational and follow-through abilities. Use facts more than you do and increase your ability to set time limits and abide by them. Also, work on improving your verbal capability.

If most of your answers were "L" answers, you possess what is known as the "engineering" mind. You are analytical, logical, organized, detailed. You solve problems pragmatically rather than creatively. And many problems do need to be solved this way. Some problems, however, require a right-brained solution. To increase your capacity to tap into this sphere, use "What if . . . ?" questions frequently. Practice drawing or painting. Learn to play a musical instrument. Try to think holistically rather than narrowly.

Exercise:

Engage in mental playfulness.

State a condition in your work environment that you feel could be improved (don't tell how to improve it; just describe the situation):

_____

_____

_____

Now look at the problem above and as you do so, allow other words to pop into your head. Write those words in column A below. They will be your first set of stimuli.

	A	B	C
1.	_____	_____	connoisseur
2.	_____	_____	collop
3.	_____	_____	compartment
4.	_____	_____	contest
5.	_____	_____	castanets
6.	_____	_____	cardinal
7.	_____	_____	collywobbles
8.	_____	_____	congregation
9.	_____	_____	cowboy
10.	_____	_____	crust
11.	_____	_____	currency
12.	_____	_____	cherub
13.	_____	_____	charisma
14.	_____	_____	circle
15.	_____	_____	conch

Next, open a dictionary and find fifteen different words—any words—on fifteen different pages. (You need *not* restrict yourself to pages from a single letter of the alphabet.) In column B, write down the first word that grabs you, whether or not you know its meaning.

Now look at your problem once again and then immediately look at the words in Columns A, B, and C. Take the words and quickly explore them mentally. One of them probably contains the nugget of a good idea, a way of solving the problem. If you still don't have a clue, give your list to a friend and ask for fifteen more freely-associated words and then re-play with the words.

Keep on doing this until you find a word or word-combination that contains the kernel of a solution. Sooner or later you'll find one that triggers a possibility, one that you previously wouldn't have considered. But you must remain open to those possibilities. If you're not capable of mental "free-falling" in the clouds of uncertainty, you will never see new horizons.

Possesses a "Shoshin" Mind-set

From Japan comes the word *shoshin,* which is defined as "a beginner's mind." Having a shoshin mind-set means looking at things anew, much as a child would—not yet having formed rigid mind-sets that limit possibilities. Sometimes experience works against us—it prevents us from taking off on flights of fancy. And without such flights, innovations remain stalled on the tarmac of the mundane.

As observed by Buddhist scholar Shunryu Suzuki, "In the beginner's mind there are many possibilities; in the expert's mind there are few." One technique that will help you view problems from a beginner's perspective is to actually ask a child, or several children if you can, how he or she would solve a given problem. The unfettered perspective, the uncluttered view born of innocence rather than experience, is often what we need to invent new realities.

Exercise:

Move beyond the known.

Read this actual letter from a secretary in a multinational company. She is thanking secretaries in the corporate office for the seminar they arranged for secretaries throughout the corporation:

Dear Nora/Christine/Lonnie:

> I just wanted to let you know that your hard work paid off. After attending the seminar, I decided I had enough confidence in myself and it was my responsibility to share this information with the other secretaries here.

> I held a briefing on Tuesday for all the secretaries (voluntary attendance). The response was overwhelming—14 of 15 secretaries attended.

> The presentation was just a brief overview taking one and a half hours. We discussed: Who we are? What we are? Where do we want to be? What can we do about it? (I used all my material from the seminar in Calabasas.) There was plenty of discussion. We could have used the whole day.

> I have enclosed a copy of the slides and handouts. (They might be of use to someone else.) Each secretary was also given a company pen, a bound notepad, and a looseleaf book with "My Job—How to do it when I am away" (adapted for our office with all our forms and general information added). These little extras were very well received.

> Starting in the new year we will have monthly meetings with pre-selected topics. We are also going to have each Director take a turn at explaining his/her department at the beginning of each meeting. We hope to have training sessions, et cetera.

I would never have imagined that I could do this. Thanks to you, Nora, Christine, and Lonnie, and especially Marlene [the seminar presenter], talking and sharing with all the other secretaries, I did it. (If I had been asked to do this six months ago, I could not have done it. I must admit it was very scary but very worthwhile.)

Many, many thanks to all of you!

"If you always do what you've always done, you'll always be what you've always been."

Barb Hutchinson

(*reprinted with permission*)

In what specific ways has this individual grown in the short period of six months? _____

_____

_____

_____

_____

_____

_____

Her letter should have given you some ideas of your own. What are they? _____

_____

_____

_____

_____

_____

_____

In your opinion, what is necessary for increasing self-confidence?

_____

_____

_____

_____

_____

Do you wish to "be what you've always been"? _____

If so, why? _____

If not—if you wish to grow beyond your current excellence—explain why. _____

_____

_____

_____

_____

_____

_____

What benefits might result—for you, for other secretaries, for your organization—if you move beyond "what you've always done"?

_____

_____

_____

_____

_____

_____

_____

Exercise:

Develop worst-case/ best-case scenarios.

As adults, we cannot realistically view the world with the same sense of wonder we did as children. We have seen too much, done too much, learned too much. But we can temporarily suspend disbelief and allow ourselves to be caught up in imaginings. As you contemplate the secretarial profession, ask if you would want your child to enter it. (Most secretaries don't.) If not, what are your reasons?

_____

_____

_____

_____

_____

_____

_____

If you _would_ want your child to become a secretary, what are your reasons? _____

_____

_____

_____

_____

_____

_____

_____

Now think about the secretarial profession ten years from now. What are the best possible conditions associated with that role? _____

_____

_____

_____

_____

_____

_____

_____

_____

What is a worst-case scenario for secretaries ten years hence? (Try not to merely supply the opposite of what you wrote above.) _____

_____

_____

_____

_____

_____

_____

_____

_____

Experts predict that the secretarial function will actually be split in the future—skilled secretaries will assume more managerial functions. Those who don't continuously update their skills will be relegated to clerical responsibilities.

And so, it seems, it will be both the best of times and the worst of times for secretaries, depending on how much of a commitment they are willing to make to continuing education.

Having reviewed both your worst-case and your best-case scenario as well, what do you need to do to ensure the latter is more likely to be part of your future?_____

_____

_____

_____

_____

_____

_____

_____

_____

_____

_____

_____

_____

_____

INTERVIEW: Janet Weissend, CPS, Administrative Assistant, Eastman Kodak Company, Rochester, New York

Q: *What is the nature of creativity?*

A: Basically, I think it means going beyond the obvious. For example, instead of just sorting the mail and deciding what my boss should receive and what I can handle, I divide his mail into eight piles ("top priority," "dated material," "reading material," et cetera). This makes it easier for both of us.

Q: *Can you give us other examples of ways you have gone beyond the obvious?*

A: I am always looking for ways to make things better. For example, I have streamlined some of our forms and have developed cross-references for some of our files. Whenever something seems unnecessarily complex, I try to simplify it.

Q: *You seem to have little hesitation proposing good ideas to your boss. But what advice would you give someone who is fearful of doing that?*

A: I'd recommend that secretaries think through their ideas very carefully. They need to develop a plan and list the benefits to the organization. It would be foolish of a boss to deny ideas that might make things better. The secretary need only say, "I would like to share this idea with you." If the boss is not receptive, the secretary should ask to implement the idea on a trial basis: "Could we try it for a month?"

Q: *How do you keep abreast of the latest management thinking?*

A: Every year I seek out relevant training programs and seminars. Afterwards, I meet with the other secretaries in our group and we review the information. In the weeks and months following the course, I will connect something I learned with something our group is working on at the moment.

Q: *Does Kodak have a company-wide thrust for innovation?*

A: Company-wide we have a strong emphasis on continuous improvement. Quality principles are important in the Kodak culture and that kind of improvement is emphasized in every department. We do have other efforts—such as the Idea Forum, a group of people who meet to brainstorm solutions to existing problems. Since the late 1970s, a Worldwide Innovation Network (WIN) has been an effective channel for employee ideas. And, of course, there are pockets of innovative thinking throughout the company—people like my boss, who encourage creativity in other people, who encourage independent thought.

Q: *What would you do to encourage imaginative thinking in a department?*

A: I would tell others to stop and think "What if...?" and "Why don't we try...?" questions. Remind people and keep reminding them of the need for such thinking. I would give examples until they started to believe in their own capacity for creative thought. I would take a piece of the idea and help them expand on it, piggyback on it, until it blossomed into something more, something new.

Q: *Do Kodak secretaries have a formal network uniting them?*

A: About two years ago, I formed an informal network of secretaries and business support professionals: K.N.E.C.T. (Kodak News-Education-Communication Team). I found that while some divisions had their own formal secretarial councils, members of smaller departments like mine often felt isolated from peers. Additionally, many of those councils focused on policies, procedures, and divisional issues rather than on professional growth.

I formed K.N.E.C.T. as a cross-division vehicle for Kodak secretaries and administrative assistants to share ideas and information and learn from one another. Today our group has a ten-member core team and a distribution list of 750 business support professionals from all parts of Kodak. Among other subjects, we've had meetings on career development, personal safety, living with change, and personality styles.

Is Willing to Escape Mental Restraints

"All behavior consists of opposites… Learn to see things backward, inside out, and upside down." Lao-tzu's statement is strong encouragement for you to think in ways that aren't natural or normal. Mind-stretching takes some work—especially at first—for it requires leaving the security of traditional mental moorings. But the creative mind is meant to pioneer, to escape the familiar and explore the unknown.

Exercise:

Discover your assumptions and then work without them.

We sometimes create shadows that prevent the light of discovery from shining through. These shadows are self-imposed limits: We often assume restraints when none exist. The following five-minute experiment illustrates this point.

If possible, work at your desk—either at home or at the office. Have a timer ready and set it for five minutes as soon as you understand the directions that follow: You are to create as many sentences as you possibly can in a five-minute period. The sentences can have only five words. The first word in every sentence must begin with the letter "A." The second word in every sentence must begin with the letter "B." The third word in every sentence must begin with the letter "C." The fourth word in every sentence must begin with the letter "D." And the last word in every sentence must begin with the letter "E." Once you have used a word, you cannot use it again.

Here are some examples: A   B   C   D   E

All beasts can dance effortlessly.

Another boy could design everything.

1. _____

2. _____

3. _____

4. _____

5. _____

6. _____

7. _____

8. _____

9. _____

10. _____

11. _____

12. _____

13. _____

14. _____

15. _____

16. _____

17. _____

18. _____

19. _____

20. _____

How did you do? Most people are able to generate five to eight sentences. (If you got as many as twenty, you are among a very rare group.) Now let's examine some assumptions. Did you assume at first that you couldn't use a dictionary? Did you actually use a dictionary? Those who wind up with a high number of sentences usually realize they aren't breaking any rules by using available resources.

Did you assume the sentences had to be "built" horizontally? Did you create horizontal or vertical sentences? Would you have been able to create more sentences if you had listed twenty "A" words, then twenty beginning with "B," and so on?

Did you assume you couldn't use proper nouns? Did you actually use them? Perhaps you could have created more sentences if you had done the task in the following way. Try it, and see whether you come up with more sentences.

First, create a column of nouns or adjectives starting with the letter "A." Once that column is complete, write twenty "B" words—verbs if you started with nouns, and nouns if you started with adjectives. In the third column, write "C" words—nouns if you started with nouns and verbs if you started with adjectives. Your fourth column will contain all "D" words and the final column, all "E" words.

As you attack problems in the future, arm yourself with as many tools as you can. One of the most effective tools is the ability to challenge or suspend your assumptions.

Exercise:

Personify your problems.

This technique taps into our infinite capacity for imagination. Caution: If you have never tried this before, you may find it difficult to slip into the territory of the imagination. There are no signposts here. Cartographers have prepared no maps. When you work with methods like this, you are exploring unfamiliar "terra," which will not become "firma" until you have returned to it several times.

1. Write down a problem you (or your organization) are facing now or will have to face in the future: _____

   _____

   _____

   _____

2. Now imagine that your problem is actually a person, a person from another time, another place. Personify your problem. Pretend that it's someone living in a different era, a different city. What sort of person do you see in your mind's eye right now? _____

   _____

   _____

3. Now list the traits/qualities/characteristics/behaviors/visuals/entities associated with that person. For example, if the problem you described in #1 were reduced budgets causing reduced training opportunities, you might view this problem as a dentist in an ultra-modern office. The aspects/items associated with such an individual could be Novocaine and listening to soothing music.

   These two characteristics alone could spark partial solutions for your problem. For example, what might lessen the pain of having fewer training opportunities? Possibly having skilled employees (instead of outside instructors) train others in informal settings. For the selected invididuals, the recognition they receive would certainly soften the blow of not attending formal classes. Listening to music might make you think of audiotapes. For a minimal fee, the company could invest in audiotapes of the leading business books. Discussion groups could subsequently be formed.

Go on now to list the traits/qualities/characteristics/behaviors/visuals/entities associated with your problem. Choose any persona except the dentist illustrated here and the sheriff used as an example in #4.

_____   _____   _____

_____   _____   _____

_____   _____   _____

_____   _____   _____

4. Now see yourself solving the problem as that person would solve the problem. To illustrate, say that you personified the problem as a sheriff in the Old West. In that era, sheriffs often formed posses. One possible solution to your problem, then, might be to join forces with a number of other people. ("There's strength in numbers.") Sheriffs wear badges, showing the law is on their side. Another possible solution to your problem could be legal precedents that would lend weight to the proposal or cause you are pursuing.

What aspects of your personified figure (your problem in disguise) might help solve this current problem? Look back to the traits you listed in #3, let your mind wander, think again about the two examples, and then explore possible solutions based on the features possessed by the persona you have chosen to represent your problem. _____

_____

_____

Sees the Big Picture

We sometimes become so immersed in the nitty-gritty that we fail to remember why we're doing the nitty-gritty to begin with. "What larger purpose is this activity serving?" is a question you should ask yourself several times each day. If there's no important bigger purpose, or if the activity doesn't relate directly to the organizational mission or your personal goals, reexamine its necessity.

Exercise:

Ask questions.

No matter how independent we think we are, we cannot work in isolation. Your work affects the work of other people. And the work of other people influences the work you do.

A. List the names of three people you depend on to do the work you're expected to do:

1. _____

2. _____

3. _____

B. Now list the names of three people who depend on you to do the work they're expected to do:

1. _____

2. _____

3. _____

C. If one of the people you listed asked you one of the following questions, how would you respond? Write your answers in the blanks.

• What benefits our customers most? _____

_____

_____

_____

• What is wasting time? _____

_____

_____

_____

- What doesn't need to be done?_____

    _____

    _____

    _____

- What is most important to the mission?_____

    _____

    _____

    _____

- What could I do to make your job easier?_____

    _____

    _____

    _____

- Other questions? _____

    _____

    _____

    _____

D. Take the initiative to meet informally with one person whose work affects your own and with another person who depends on you. Ask each other the questions in Section C. What innovations or improvements might result from such a meeting?

_____

_____

_____

_____

_____

Exercise:

Look for resources from within.

You know yourself well, but you probably don't really know the heights you're capable of reaching. The life of the average secretary is a busy one—both inside and outside the office. As a result, there's little time for introspection. Typically, we don't plumb our inner depths unless we're forced to. Try the following exercise to get a handle on who you think you are.

A. As quickly as you can, jot down ten adjectives to describe yourself. Use words that reflect attitudes, emotions, and capability rather than ones that describe physical traits ("intelligent" rather than "tall" for example). Write the first ten that pop into your head:

1. _____

2. _____

3. _____

4. _____

5. _____

6. _____

7. _____

8. _____

9. _____

10. _____

Did you find it difficult to describe yourself? Most people do. Even though you have lived with yourself for twenty or thirty years or more, you may not ever have assessed yourself in this way. One interesting experiment is to ask others who know you well to write down ten nonphysical adjectives that describe you. Compare the list and analyze the discrepancies.

Others no doubt will see things in you that you don't see in yourself. And there will be those who fail to see some things that you might feel are the essential you. As the ancient Greeks told us, "The unexamined life is not worth living." Periodically examine yourself and your life so that you can enjoy both more fully.

As you complete the second half of this exercise, *don't look* at the list of adjective you just jotted down on the preceding page.

B. Now create a list of ten nonphysical adjectives that describe you— the first ten that pop into your head—but this time, write with your opposite hand!

1. _____

2. _____

3. _____

4. _____

5. _____

6. _____

7. _____

8. _____

9. _____

10. _____

Compare your two lists now. In theory, they should be the same—you wrote about the same subject—one you know very well—and you made the second list just minutes after composing the first. The only difference was that you switched the pen from one hand to the other. (The lists are seldom identical.)

What did you learn about yourself? _____

_____

_____

_____

_____

_____

_____

_____

Is Able to Withstand Rejection and Failure

Success seldom comes to those unwilling to progress beyond their first failure. It's the ability to withstand rejection that separates successful dreamers from unsuccessful ones. If you have a good idea, you must protect it from outside forces that could easily destroy it. If you have faith in your abilities, you must make yourself less vulnerable to criticism.

Be encouraged by three guests who once appeared on David Susskind's talk show. All three were self-made millionaires by their mid-thirties. They had one thing in common—they averaged eighteen failures in nonsuccessful ventures before they finally met with success. Use such stories to buoy your spirits when support for your idea is disappearing.

Helen Keller certainly possessed the ability to regard setbacks as successes lurking incognito: "When one door of opportunity closes, another opens; but often we look so long at the closed door that we do not see the one which has been opened for us."

As thinking people, we always have choices. We can choose to remain mired in current failure or we can rise above it to head toward future achievements. It is fairly easy to complain—particularly if the past grievance was undeserved. It is harder to do something constructive about the complaint, to move on to a solution instead of remaining in the bog of accusation. Which sort of person are you? Do you savor the flavor of despair? Or do you prefer turning "lemons" into metaphorical "lemonade"?

Exercise:

Find a "failure hero" and let that person be your guide.

Can you identify this person?

When he was 22, his business failed.

When he was 23, he was defeated in his bid for the legislature.

When he was 24, he experienced another business failure.

When he was 25, he was successful in his efforts to be elected to the legislature.

When he was 26, the woman he loved died.

When he was 27, he suffered a nervous breakdown.

When he was 29, he was denied a chance to be a speaker.

When he was 31, he lost a bid to be an elector.

When he was 34, he ran for Congress and was defeated.

When he was 37, he was successful in running for Congress.

When he was 39, he mounted an unsuccessful campaign for Congress.

When he was 46, he was defeated in his efforts to become a senator.

When he was 47, he experienced failure in his vice-presidential efforts.

When he was 49, he was defeated in his attempt to become a senator.

When he was 51, he was chosen to be President of the United States of America.

This remarkably persistent person was Abraham Lincoln, a true "failure hero." Find another—perhaps by interviewing someone in your own organization—and write that person's record in a manner similar to the one above. Keep that record posted and turn to it for inspiration.

Exercise:

Test your "flopportunity" quotient.

This simple test will give you an indication of your willingness to let a setback turn into a flop or into an opportunity. If you are easily discouraged, if mistakes make you feel unworthy, if you cannot see beyond today's darkness into tomorrow's sunlight—then the opportunity will disintegrate and the temporary failure will assume an importance it doesn't deserve.

On the other hand, if you can persevere, if you can view rejection as a step in the path of success, if you really can train yourself to hope eternally, then quite possibly the flop will become an opportunity.

Check the blank ("Yes" or "No") that best reflects your response to each question. Be as honest with yourself as possible—no one else will see your answers.

Yes ___ No ___   1. Little things tend to upset me.

Yes ___ No ___   2. I have an extensive support network.

Yes ___ No ___   3. I enjoy hearing success stories, especially if they began in adversity.

Yes ___ No ___   4. I believe in self-indulgence on occasion.

Yes ___ No ___   5. I would define myself as a pessimist.

Yes ___ No ___   6. I remember to appreciate each day.

Yes ___ No ___   7. I can shut out negative thoughts.

Yes ___ No ___   8. I believe most clouds have silver linings.

Yes ___ No ___   9. I equate failure with humiliation.

Yes ___ No ___   10. I believe I have control over my life.

Yes ___ No ___   11. I usually depend on others to effect change.

Yes ___ No ___   12. I feel fortunate to be/have what I am/have.

Yes ___ No ___   13. I tend to envy the circumstances of others.

Score your responses using this chart.

 1. "yes," -10 points; "no," +10 points

 2. "yes," +10 points; "no," -10 points

 3. "yes," +10 points; "no," -10 points

 4. "yes," +10 points; "no," -10 points

 5. "yes," -10 points; "no," +10 points

 6. "yes," +10 points; "no," -10 points

 7. "yes," +10 points; "no," -10 points

 8. "yes," +10 points; "no," -10 points

 9. "yes," -10 points; "no," +10 points

10. "yes," +10 points; "no," -10 points

11. "yes," -10 points; "no," +10 points

12. "yes," +10 points; "no," -10 points

13. "yes," -10 points; "no," +10 points

If you scored 80+ points, there's a very strong possibility that you can convert flops to "ops." You are realistic enough to know that while every cloud may have a silver lining, the very existence of clouds means some rain will fall into your life. But you are aware of choices—you can either be drenched by the deluge or can splash about a bit and then go indoors to get warm.

If you scored below 80, you may wish to take stock of the many blessings you have. And look back over the times of adversity and remind yourself of how much better you are for having experienced them.

Is Willing to Persevere

Perseverance has been defined as the "eternal try-angle." How would you define it? Perhaps more important, do you agree with the definition of a "try-angle"? When life knocks you down—and it will— have you the courage and persistance to get right back up? Secretaries who have good ideas that aren't initially accepted know they can either abandon the idea or resubmit it. Losers give up; winners keep on trying. Eventually, with enough trys and even trials, the idea will gain acceptance. (Even if it does not, you will be admired for your "do-or-die" attitude.) Creative ideas need you to fight on their behalf. Be an idea-warrior, knowing that you won't win every battle but you will win the war, the war against complacency.

Exercise:

Gauge your ability to persevere rather than perseverate.

There is a distinction between persevering and perseverating. And a very simple experiment will tell you which you are more inclined to do. From the following sentence, one letter of the alphabet has been removed—from 11 places in the sentence. You can probably figure out the missing letter fairly quickly. But can you figure out the sentence?

VRYVNINGLLNATSLDRBRRYPI.

When you have finished, review your thinking process and answer these questions:

1. What word did you begin with? _____

_____

_____

_____

2. If you began with the word "very," approximately how long did you stay with it? _____

_____

_____

_____

3. Did you feel frustrated when you could not get it to "fit" into the rest of the sentence? _____

_____

_____

_____

4. Were you annoyed or challenged by the prospect of finding another first word? _____

_____

_____

_____

_____

5. If you began with the word "every," how long did it take you to realize you were on the right track? _____

_____

_____

_____

_____

6. Did you look at the whole line first, trying to figure out individual words, or did you start at the beginning and try to figure out individual words? _____

_____

_____

_____

_____

The sentence, of course, is "Every evening Ellen eats elderberry pie." Although the missing letter "e" may have been obvious to you, you probably had to make several efforts to learn where the words divided. People who "perseverate" continue a behavior even if the desired effect is not being achieved. Those who "persevere" do not engage in repetitive behavior unless it is leading them to a goal. Clearly, it is better to persevere, to have the stick-to-it-ive-ness that helps us ultimately achieve the goals we have set for ourselves.

Exercise:

Use several "doors" to gain entry.

"Don't argue about difficulties. The difficulties will argue for themselves." The words of Winston Churchill apply equally well to individuals or teams. We often allow problems to assume the driver's seat and lead us to dead ends. We focus so intensively on the negative that we don't give positives a chance to be seen or heard.

Creative employees, by contrast, know that if obvious answers aren't attainable, there are less-obvious answers that may serve as well or nearly as well. If the front door doesn't allow access to the solution, they will try other doors and even windows to gain entry.

To illustrate, assume your dream is to play in the National Basketball Association (NBA). But your size and your sex make that dream impossible to attain. Rather than closing the door on the NBA-nexus, you might consider a related job. There are no doubt more than you realized:

Coach	Director of Publications and Information
Assistant Coach	Video Coordinator
Business Manager	Scout
Director of Marketing	Team Physician
Director of Administration	Strength and Conditioning Coach
Director of Community Relations	Trainer
Director of Scouting Services	Assistant Trainer
Director of Public Relations	Executive Director
Basketball Consultant	Manager of Community Programs
Choreographer	Manager of Cheerleaders
Cheerleader	Manager of Promotions

Now, write down one of your goals: _____

_____

_____

_____

_____

_____

What obstacles are keeping you from that goal? _____

_____

_____

_____

_____

_____

What other doors could you walk through in order to achieve that
goal? _____

_____

_____

_____

_____

_____

_____

_____

Is Self-Confident About Ideas

We all have good ideas. Some of us, though, are more willing to fight for them than others are. Think about the last good idea you had. What happened to it? What *typically* happens to your ideas?

Often, ideas are born of faith and need faith to sustain them until they reach maturity. After all, the Wright brothers only *thought* their plane would fly—they had no proof. And so it goes with discoveries both physical and cerebral—if not for the confidence the idea-proposer has in him- or herself and in the capacity of others to follow through, good ideas might only be fleeting thoughts.

Exercise:

Prepare a "birth" announcement.

Imagine you have been asked to write a birth announcement (or a "worth" announcement) for a good idea you or your team recently had. By publicly proclaiming a well-researched proposal, you can often garner support that helps you sustain the faith you have in the innovation.

You may use the accompanying form or one that you create yourself. Either way, the form should serve as a succinct means of advising others of your efforts to continuously bring improvement. In fact, you may wish to mention that you're working on such a form and would like to share it with them in the future in order to facilitate communication. Then, when you've done your homework, simply fill out the form and distribute it.

Announcing

Idea: _____

_____

Cost: _____

Benefits: _____

Precedents: _____

Who will be affected: _____

Approval required: _____

When to start: _____

Comments: _____

Submitted by: _____ Date: _____

Is Self-Confident About Ideas

Exercise:

Keep a log to chart the progress of your ideas.

Records can help you understand what went wrong and what went right with the ideas you propose. Your charting need not be complex (it can be as simple as the sample Idea Tracker on the next page), but it should help you trace the history of your innovative proposals so you can learn which stumbling blocks may have destroyed the confidence you initially felt in your idea. Begin with your most recent good idea.

IDEA TRACKER

Idea: _____

Date: _____

Efforts I made to implement it:_____

_____

_____

Results of those efforts: _____

_____

_____

What I learned that will be useful next time: _____

_____

_____

What I will avoid next time: _____

_____

_____

INTERVIEW: Loralee Pearson, Director of Secretarial Services, Nu Skin International, Provo, Utah

Q: *Director of Secretarial Services itself is an innovation. How was your job created?*

A: Five years ago, I was hired by Nu Skin for a position as supervisor for the secretaries and receptionists. It was an adventure for me because I knew very little about Nu Skin International. In time, I became Director of Secretarial Services, a new position with the company. Management has given me free reign to develop my department as I have desired to stay abreast of the company's rapid growth. Because they have shown this faith, I have taken seriously the need to do the best job possible.

Q: *What innovations have you instituted?*

A: My employees are cross-trained to fulfill multiple assignments. I have telephone receptionists who answer all incoming calls to the general phone lines and direct calls between departments inside the company. There is a secretary on each floor in the reception area who, in addition to acting as a receptionist, serves as a general secretary for anyone on that floor needing secretarial assistance.

I have formed a typing center/substitute pool that does overflow typing for any person or department who requests it. The typing center will do letters, transcribe audiotapes, take and type meeting minutes, and do special mailings, labels, spreadsheets, data entry, charts, graphics, and so on. The people in the secretarial pool will substitute for department secretaries, floor secretaries, and other clerical positions when needed, whether for an hour or for a six-week maternity leave.

My department personnel act as daily tour guides for the new high-rise building.

Recently I added a records management specialist to help set up the filing system of any department or employee who requests help. I have a trainer who helps with new-employee orientation and periodic in-service training as well.

We keep the corporate telephone directories current. With eight hundred employees in this building and four hundred at our local distribution center, there are constant changes. We have a telephone directory on the computer network. We will provide a flip-chart directory for executives, directors, and secretaries who request it. We also make a general directory by department, and an alphabetical directory by employees' first names. We recently purchased a directory assistance program, which lists all telephone numbers for the United States. Our employees can call our department for this assistance rather than the area phone company, thus saving the company approximately $400 to $500 each month.

Q: *What lessons have you learned over the years that would benefit other secretaries?*

A: I had no previous experience with this company, nor had they ever needed someone to oversee their secretarial/receptionist staff. Consequently, it was a learning experience for me. The creativity they have allowed me in developing my own department has been enjoyable and invigorating. I found you must do more than just depend on textbook knowledge. Leadership and interpersonal skills are very important. I do think it's important to train employees properly.

In my own department, telephone training is important. Not only training in the functions of the phone systems but also training in phone etiquette. Customer service is critical—being friendly, helpful, and really listening to people's needs. Tour guides must be able to interact and communicate well with other people, in addition to having a comprehensive knowledge of the company and its products.

Seminars and in-service training are necessary for keeping service at a high level. We strongly endorse cross-training.

Another item of critical importance is having a good attitude. People want to be served by a knowledgeable and gracious individual. Being a support department for the entire company, we believe in saying "yes," in doing whatever we can to make the company function more effectively and efficiently. I discourage the "No," "I-don't-have-time," or the "I-can't" attitude.

Secretaries should be flexible, adaptable, have a good attitude, and continually try to upgrade training and education. And, of course, it's important to network.

Q: *What advice would you give to secretaries who view their employment as a "dead-end" job?*

A: One needs to look at the position and determine if it is or can become satisfactory. If there is work in a company that needs to be done and it falls within a person's capacity, then he or she should do it. And if one can't or if the position does not allow for expansion, then be wise enough to move on. I am a willing mentor for any employee who has aspirations beyond my department.

Is Willing to Let Ideas Incubate

Yes, it is possible to be spontaneously imaginative—to spin off a dozen ideas in the blink of an eye. It's also possible to let your subconscious grapple with a problem over a period of hours or days or even weeks. When you let your ideas "incubate," you usually produce more sophisticated ones that become solutions to more complex problems. Let your subconscious go to work for you. At night, before you retire, think about a problem you're facing or a situation you'd like to make better. During your sleeping hours, your subconscious will actually wrestle with the problem and, in time, will find an answer.

Exercise:

Immunize yourself against "imagicides."

There will always be those who, deliberately or inadvertently, will engage in "imagicide"—they will attempt to "kill your imaginings," to strangle your good ideas.

You've heard these killer phrases—perhaps you've even used some yourself:

"Just do your work. We don't pay you to think."

"We've tried it before."

"It'll never work."

"Management will never approve it."

"It costs too much."

"That's a dumb idea."

Your idea, in a sense, owes its life to you. But you have some responsibility too. A parent gives birth but cannot subsequently abandon the child. Similarly, once you have given birth to a good idea, you are expected to sustain it, to give it life—at least until you reach the point where you must give the idea a proper burial. But give it time to incubate and grow first.

How can you immunize yourself during the gestation period?

- *Anticipate "imagicides."* Make yourself mentally ready for the comments you are bound to hear and tell yourself you are strong enough to withstand any and all of them.

- *Keep a diary of successful ideas you've proposed in the past.* You don't need to memorize this material, but "know" what's on it so you can offer concrete examples of past success to offset the force of future criticism.

- *Ask a question of the idea-slayer.* For example, "Why don't you think it will work?" "What would you propose instead?" "Did you forget that management is actively seeking our ideas?"

- *Ask to implement the idea for a trial period.* If you have paved the way sufficiently, the idea should enjoy some measure of success. You can then ask to extend the trial period to make the idea standard operating procedure.

- *Obtain the support of someone in the organization who is well respected.* When appropriate, let others know you have the endorsement of someone in management.

- *Find precedents, either in your organization's history or in the history of comparable organizations.* People are more willing to try new ideas if they know those ideas have been tried in other places.

- *Make certain you've played devil's advocate with your own idea.* Be prepared to defend it by deflecting the negative comments. Be certain, too, to have at your fingertips persuasive facts and figures that present the benefits that will accrue if your idea is adopted.

Like parenthood, self-defense and idea defense are not easy. But the maturing of the seeds into fruit is well worth the effort.

Exercise:

Create a climate conducive to incubation.

What happens to a good idea immediately after it's popped into your head? What's the climate you've created for sustaining it? Complete the following sentences to make you more aware of the mental environment in which your imaginings thrive or expire. Place an "X" beside the response in the middle or right-hand column, whichever most resembles the reality of your life.

1. My work space is like	☐ a monastery	☐ a kindergarten
2. My verbal style is like	☐ a librarian's	☐ a circus performer's
3. My documentation is like	☐ a bank	☐ a jazz score written on a paper napkin
4. My thinking style is like	☐ a Japanese garden	☐ Disneyworld
5. My concentration ability is like	☐ hopscotch	☐ Ping-Pong
6. My perseverance is like	☐ a hothouse flower	☐ a weed
7. My self-confidence is like	☐ air	☐ concrete
8. My personality is like	☐ skiing	☐ stamp collecting
9. My goals are like	☐ a kitten	☐ a tiger
10. My attitude toward life is like	☐ Sunday school	☐ a martial arts class

11. My willingness to stand up for myself is like ☐ the Constitution ☐ a handshake

12. My non-work life is like ☐ a dream ☐ a nightmare

13. My creative ability is like ☐ summer vacation ☐ the Christmas holidays

14. My communication style is like ☐ Abraham Lincoln ☐ W.C. Fields

15. My decision-making style is like ☐ pin the tail on the donkey ☐ a love sonnet

Only you can interpret what your forced-choice answers mean. As you review your "X" choices, describe the general environments—both interior and exterior—that are part of your life: _____

_____

_____

_____

_____

_____

_____

_____

_____

_____

_____

_____

_____

Finally, answer these questions about your environments and the ideas that are born in them.

1. As you think about your interior environment, would you agree it contains the serenity required for ideas to incubate? _____ If "yes," what good ideas have "hatched" lately as the result of quiet and perhaps even subconscious incubation? _____

   _____

   _____

   _____

   If "no," what can you do to de-stress your mind?_____

   _____

   _____

2. As you think about your exterior environment, would you agree it is both organized and yet stimulating so ideas can percolate without danger of evaporating?_____ If "yes," what parts of your work environment do you feel are most beneficial to idea-incubation? How can you increase or enhance those areas?

   _____

   _____

   If "no," ask a colleague's advice on how to organize your workstation better and yet keep it appealing and interesting. Record the advice below.

   _____

   _____

   _____

   _____

   _____

   _____

Is
Resourceful

The imaginative employee avoids wailing and hand wringing. Instead of complaining about resources that aren't available, the resourceful individual uses what is available and uses it well. Necessity, after all, is the mother of invention. As William McGowan, CEO of MCI Communications, has wisely commented: "Significant progress doesn't come from the formal planning process of an American corporation. It comes from a couple of guys doing something that hasn't been set down on a list."

There is much to be said for formality—of planning processes and other structured, proven techniques. However, the organization that understands the haphazardness of spontaneous creativity knows that good ideas can come at any time, in any place, to anyone.

112

Exercise:

Look within and without.

In a famous experiment involving resourcefulness, students in an engineering class at a major university were given this assignment (can you figure it out?):

The students were given one hour to remove two Ping-Pong balls from the bottom of a narrow metal cylinder that had been bolted to the floor of their science lab. They could not leave the classroom (to obtain a vacuum cleaner, for example), but they were free to use anything in the lab (such as bubblegum they might have been chewing).

The engineering students failed to find a solution—even though it was right in front of them all along: They could have filled the cylinder with water and the Ping-Ping balls would have *floated* to the top. Water was in the room; likewise talents are within each employee. If the water isn't noticed, it won't be turned on.

But if bosses aren't able to see or discover the inner resources employees have, and/or if employees aren't able to assess their own strengths, the resources will not be used. With that in mind, answer the following questions to identify the "resources" that are within you. Good ideas are truly all around us and within us!

What do you feel is the greatest contribution you can make to your organization? _____

_____

_____

_____

When is the last time someone asked you the above question? _____

_____

_____

What would your boss say is the greatest contribution you can make or are making to the organization? _____

_____

_____

_____

_____

Would you be willing to ask your boss this question and then to see how closely his or her answer matches your own?_____

_____

_____

_____

_____

_____

In every organization, valuable resources, including human resources, are overlooked and underused. But you can change that reality with a modicum of effort.

Exercise:

Establish communities to broaden your resources.

Secretaries who want to make a difference know the process is facilitated when people work together. Witness EAGLES—an Empowered Action Group Leading and Excelling in Support. This group from the Franciscan Health System of Cincinnati, Inc., began in August 1993, when a Quality Action Team asked them to "meet on a regular basis to establish procedures and to create an atmosphere for coordinating and standardizing management support functions by promoting communication, teamwork, and empowerment."

These five support staff members, in addition to their regular work, participate in a number of activities, including the quarterly publication of the *EAGLES Express*. In the very first issue were articles about empowerment, surveys, and available courses, as well as information about equipment and about a local grammar hotline. The EAGLES have established both micro and macro communities within their organization in an effort to improve quality and productivity.

Think about your own organization as a pie. What core values represent the cohesive crust? To what beliefs about the organization do virtually all employees subscribe? _____

_____

_____

_____

_____

_____

Divide up this organizational pie into the major departments or functions of your workplace:

Which departments could you form an alliance with to improve processes and/or products? Place an "A" in that slice of the pie. Work within the secretarial community to find alliance members.

Has an Entrepreneurial Spirit

Achievement is a vital aspect of the entrepreneurial spirit. Setting one's own challenges and experiencing the thrill of victory or the agony of defeat—on an individual basis—drive the entrepreneur. The innovative secretary is not "Stepford secretary." (*The Stepford Wives* was a novel by Ira Levin in which women were made into automatons so they could become perfect wives.) Certainly, a capable secretary will do what is asked, but at the same time continuously try to improve the existing and perhaps even challenge the established. In spirit, the creative secretary responds to the Tom Peters' declaration: "The only way you can fail these days is not to try stuff."

Creativity drives the most successful secretaries. They "try stuff." And when the stuff doesn't succeed, they try new stuff, again and again, until they realize their goals.

117

Exercise:

Assess yourself.

For each item, place an "X" in the column that best represents where you are in terms of independent thought or adventurous spirit:

1. ☐ Need to have exact details on how to do things
☐ No real preference
☐ Prefer to figure things out for myself

2. ☐ Never contradict
☐ In the middle
☐ Will speak up as necessary

3. ☐ Like to "paint by number"
☐ No real preference
☐ Prefer to make my own creations

4. ☐ Like to visit favorite places
☐ No real preference
☐ Prefer to visit places I have never been

5. ☐ Like to imitate the success of others
☐ No real preference
☐ Prefer to have others imitate my successes

6. ☐ Enjoy being able to depend on others
☐ No real preference
☐ Prefer to be independent

7. ☐ Would like to marry a millionaire
☐ Either would be fine
☐ Prefer to earn $1 million on my own

8. ☐ Read the end of a mystery first
☐ Do both
☐ Prefer to figure it out instead of peeking

9. ☐ Buy things (food, clothes, jewelry, cards)
☐ No real preference
☐ Prefer to make things

10. ☐ Feel comfortable with limited choices
☐ No real preference
☐ Prefer to consider multiple choices

There are no right or wrong, good or bad answers here. The only question is this: How mentally independent do you wish to be? If you wish to view yourself as mentally independent (and you need such a descriptor if you are to generate novel ideas), then the majority of your "X's" should be in the right-hand column. If you do wish to be regarded as having this entrepreneurial spirit but a majority of your answers fell in the left-hand column, then you need to develop self-confidence through self-challenges.

Try:

- *Engaging in small projects with limited liability.* Offer ideas that have few negative or minor negative consequences. As you gain confidence, you can propose possibilities that will have greater benefits and (usually) greater attendant risks.

- *Asking for new projects.* Suggest, for a change, that the boss allow you to figure out the best way to do a project. If the outcome of the project isn't as good as he or she had expected, you can revert back to the usual process of the boss directing and you following. If you are already at this stage, move on to the next—ask for new assignments instead of waiting for them to be given to you.

- *Logging your accomplishments.* Keep a small notebook to track the success of your entrepreneurial efforts. Ideally, you will have many more successes than failures. Use the successes to remind you of your competence whenever you are in a situation that calls for innovation; use the failures to remind you of the lessons you've learned.

- *Generating multiple options.* Train yourself to avoid "either/or" choices. Instead, offer yourself multiple options and choose the best from a wide array.

- *Brainstorming.* Employ brainstorming or mindmapping (visual free association) frequently to unlock the ideas waiting to spring forth.

- *Obtaining feedback.* Self-opinion is one way to assess the worth of ideas—either in the embryonic stage or in the innovation/ implementation stage. But the opinions of others can also be a valuable source of evaluation and information. Add one person a month to your feedback circle.

Exercise:

Dare to do.

Here is a list of activities secretaries can easily initiate to improve the workplace. Check one and then describe what you would do to make this entrepreneurial effort a success. Of course, if you'd rather undertake a project that's not listed here, go right ahead.

My choice:

- ☐ Attend a seminar for secretaries and share information with others afterward
- ☐ Plan a special event for Professional Secretaries Week
- ☐ Create a directory that lists the special expertises of various secretaries
- ☐ Put out a manual for newly hired secretaries
- ☐ Offer to teach a course for other secretaries
- ☐ Publish a newsletter just for support staff
- ☐ Establish (or improve) the company library
- ☐ Plan a multicultural event to highlight the diversity in your workplace
- ☐ Make a presentation at a secretarial conference
- ☐ Write an article for a secretarial magazine
- ☐ Form a community alliance in your organization
- ☐ Initiate a recycling effort
- ☐ Plan a conference for support staff
- ☐ Have an office-wide or organization-wide "Clean-out-the-Files" day
- ☐ Benchmark with secretaries in other organizations

☐ Other _____

_____

To make this project successful, I will have to: _____

_____

_____

_____

_____

_____

_____

_____

_____

_____

Dislikes Routine

There are people (thank goodness) who enjoy routine work. They take comfort in the familiarity and the predictability of the work expected of them. They like the unchanging repetition of their tasks and take pleasure in the perfunctory nature of their responsibilities.

Others, though, prefer work that is varied. They dislike routine and thrive instead on having "no two days alike." They aren't disturbed by the irregular pattern of their days. Indeed, they find the kaleidoscopic nature of their work exciting. There are secretaries who truly do work well under pressure. They feel exhilarated when phones ring and co-workers or customers stop by—each ring and each visitor with a new piece of that day's jigsaw puzzle, perhaps a new opportunity or an unexpected solution to a problem.

The willingness to welcome the unpredicted is what separates the innovative secretary from the merely competent one.

124

Exercise:

Be challenged by chaos.

When you look at the following picture, you probably begin to feel sensory overload. It is extremely "busy"—with many visual images competing for your attention. The chaos, however, can produce a fount of novel thought. As you study this collage, allow your mind to wander and allow the images to impinge upon your consciousness. Let the graphic stimuli wash over you as you think about some contribution you could make to the secretarial profession. Do not fear "weird" ideas. (Tom Peters recommends having at least one "weirdo" on staff!) The purpose of this exercise is to practice finding creative ideas in the midst of daily chaos.

In terms of contributions you could make to the secretarial profession, what new thoughts did the images on the preceding page inspire in you? _____

_____

_____

_____

_____

_____

_____

_____

_____

_____

_____

_____

_____

_____

_____

_____

_____

_____

_____

_____

_____

_____

Dislikes Routine

What additional "weird" thoughts have you had regarding your work
or your profession? Which of those could be "tamed" into a workable
idea? _____

_____

_____

_____

_____

_____

_____

_____

_____

_____

_____

_____

_____

_____

_____

_____

_____

_____

_____

_____

_____

Exercise:

Apply the 80/20 rule.

"When you are through changing," someone once observed, "you're through." Imaginative secretaries offer living examples of lifelong learning. They continuously assess what they're doing in order to maximize results. They constantly look for ways to improve so that waste can be minimized. They automatically consider how work is done so efforts can be optimized.

One specific technique that often helps identify duplication or non-value-added work is called the "80/20 rule." Quite simply, it states that 20 percent of the contributing factors yield 80 percent of the result. For example, if you are a salesperson with ten accounts, two of those accounts will produce the majority (about 80 percent) of your income. These two accounts—referred to as the "vital few"— should receive most of your attention. But often, the novice will divide his or her time equally among the ten accounts—despite the fact that some have a much greater return than others.

A. To determine the "vital few" and the "trivial many" in terms of your work responsibilities, list here all the tasks you are expected to complete in a given week. In other words, what does your job entail? What do you do all day long?

1. _____

2. _____

3. _____

4. _____

5. _____

6. _____

7. _____

8. _____

9. _____

10. _____

11. _____

12. _____

13. _____

14. _____

15. _____

16. _____

17. _____

18. _____

19. _____

20. _____

B. As you look over your list, identify the three tasks that you consider most important and/or that your boss would view as the most vital and/or that the head of the organization would regard as most supportive of the mission.

    1. _____

    2. _____

    3. _____

C. Approximately how much of your time do you spend on these three things? _____

D. As you look over the "trivial many," which of them could be

- Eliminated? _____

  _____

- Streamlined? _____

  _____

- Combined? _____
  _____

- Redesigned? _____
  _____

- Delegated? _____
  _____

- Traded off? _____
  _____

- Modified? _____
  _____

- Performed less often? _____
  _____

- Performed less thoroughly? _____
  _____

- Made a shared responsibility? _____
  _____

Consider what Mary DeVito, Administrative Assistant for Long Term Care at Park Ridge Hospital (in Greece, New York) was able to accomplish by asking some of these very questions:

- To reduce the amount of time spent on copying and distribution, she developed routing slips for the nursing home administrator to use in disseminating information to staff.

- To ensure that phones are covered at all times, the telephones for the Administration Department are call-forwarded to the Information Desk at the end of the day to provide coverage until 9 p.m. Additionally, the Information Desk telephones are call-forwarded to Administration from 8:00 a.m. to 8:30 a.m. since Information Desk employees don't begin their workday until 8:30 a.m.

- For years, folders were used for all board and board committee meeting packets. To save costs, she approached the CEO for his approval in eliminating the folders and using paper clips instead. The cost variance was $.25 for one hundred clips versus $11.31 for twenty-five folders (she normally ordered fifty folders each month for her meetings alone, plus in the Health System, there were approximately twenty regular meetings per month.) She shared this information with all the secretaries, and folders were eliminated for meetings throughout the Health System.

Is Able to Handle Multiple Assignments

Does this sound like anyone you know?

A secretary began her day by looking at the incoming mail. The first letter she opened was from a vendor, who used a word she'd never heard before. She looked the word up in the dictionary and then realized the dictionary cover was a bit soiled. She got up to get soap and water from the restroom but while she was there, she noticed she'd forgotten to apply lipstick that morning. Of course, she had to return to her desk to get the lipstick and then return to the restroom to use the mirror. A colleague came in, and the two began speaking about an upcoming conference. The colleague asked the secretary to fax her a copy of the program for the conference. When she returned to her desk, she went through her files and located the program, but she didn't have the fax number for her colleague. She called the receptionist to find it and was reminded that today was the day the computer class was being held. The secretary tried to

find her registration form for the computer class but couldn't. She decided to call the training department to see if she had in fact registered. The moment she hung up the phone, she remembered that she still hadn't sent the fax. As she got up to go to the fax machine, she noticed that her "file pile" was growing to a precarious height. She began to file the paper when she saw...

The ability to handle several different things simultaneously is a feature of the creative personality. To illustrate, many authors can work on three different books in a given day. To be writing five or six books simultaneously, to have concurrent works-in-progress, is not unusual among those who write for a living. Such a work style, though, would cause circuits to overload in some individuals. Can you increase your tolerance for handling multiple projects simultaneously? Yes—but only if you wish to do so. The key is to find a balance by being disciplined and organized and by learning to prioritize. The following two exercises will provide you with some practice.

Exercise:

Assess your working style.

Answer the following questions to learn more about your working style—are you mono-focused or multi-focused? Check "yes" or "no" in response to each question:

Yes ___ No ___   1. Do you prefer a "monochromatic" look to your attire?

Yes ___ No ___   2. Do you rearrange the furniture in your home or office at least once every six months?

Yes ___ No ___   3. Do you try out a new recipe from a cookbook at least once a month?

Yes ___ No ___   4. Do you use "waiting" time to do something else? (For example, do you read while waiting in line?)

Yes ___ No ___   5. Do you get annoyed by interruptions such as a phone call?

Yes ___ No ___   6. Do you feel you have improved your mind in the last week?

Yes ___ No ___   7. Do you know what kind of learner you are?

Yes ___ No ___   8. Do you finish one project before starting another?

Yes ___ No ___   9. Do you frequently have the radio or television on while you work?

Yes ___ No ___   10. Do you believe you could excel in several different types of jobs?

Give yourself ten points for every "yes" answer you had except for questions #1, #5, and #8 (allow no points for your answer to these three questions—no matter what your answer was).

Your score? _____

A score of "70" means you're quite facile at handling multiple interests at virtually the same time. This is a trait of creative people and also a trait of successfully busy people. Life is seldom so accommodating that it gives us the luxury of doing only one thing at a time. We are usually bombarded with demands—the demands of time, of people, of life itself. It would be wonderful to be able to neatly pigeonhole each responsibility, finish it with a flourish, and then move on in lockstep fashion to the next responsibility. But such a schedule is an unrealistic one. Learn to adjust to interruptions, learn to juggle multiple priorities, learn to accommodate multiple bosses. The next exercise provides a tool for doing just that.

Exercise:

Make IT a priority.

The IT technique forces you to think of two significant aspects of your working day: Intentions and Time. Begin by making a list of all the things you intend to do today. Separate your Intentions list according to things you intend to do and the calls you intend to make.

Things to do   **Calls to make**

1. _____   _____
2. _____   _____
3. _____   _____
4. _____   _____
5. _____   _____
6. _____   _____
7. _____   _____
8. _____   _____
9. _____   _____
10. _____   _____

Now let the Time factor help you prioritize. What *must* you do today? What will you do if time permits?

Use the diagram on the following page to help you sort it all out.

Must DO Today	Must CALL Today
DO if Time Allows	CALL if Time Allows

INTERVIEW: Luanne Strasenburgh, Executive Assistant to the Chairman and CEO, Bausch & Lomb, Rochester, New York

Q: *Innovation has been called "the number one management issue" of the 1990s, and it's an issue beyond the area of management as well. In addition to innovative abilities, what else should a competent secretary have?*

A: She needs strong organizational skills, common sense, communication skills, and familiarity with the community so she can serve as a political liaison.

Q: *How would you describe your own working style?*

A: It's a quick and efficient style. I like to get to the point. The phrase "no muss, no fuss" certainly applies to me. I pride myself on being businesslike but polite and friendly at the same time.

Q: *What advice would you give to the secretary who lacks these skills?*

A: There are numerous seminars for virtually any skill one needs to acquire. In fact, there are so many offerings that sometimes it is difficult to find the right one. In addition, one could work with the Human Resources or training department if the organization has such a department.

The secretary interested in self-improvement needs to determine areas of strength and weakness. She needs a willingness to self-assess and then to plan and set goals.

Q: *Why is knowledge of the community so important?*

A: By "community," I mean both the communities within the organization—such as the community of secretaries—and also the larger community outside the company. Bausch & Lomb is very active with community groups such as the Rochester Philharmonic Orchestra, GEVA Theater, many community arts programs, and education. We donate not only money, but people-time as well.

Q: *What is your approach to solving problems?*

A: I take pride in trying to solve them on my own. However, ego trips can cause problems—there is a danger in trying to do everything yourself. I know I don't know everything and I am never embarrassed to ask for help from other people when I need it. Over the years, I have had many opportunities to learn that two or even three heads are better than one.

I accept advice and I also accept criticism, for I know it might help me to perform my job even better than I do.

Q: *How would you describe your partnership with your CEO?*

A: I work very hard at being an asset to my boss. I try to be his eyes and his ears, to pay attention to both the small picture and the big picture. By dealing with the minutiae, I create more time for him to focus on the serious responsibilities that constitute his job.

Q: *What advice would you give to secretaries just entering the profession?*

A: Again, organizational skills are vital. So too are people skills. Finally, I would emphasize writing skills. Most secretaries who reach the level of executive assistant are expected to be able to draft correspondence for their bosses. And, being visible—doing excellent work that gets noticed—is usually of benefit to career-minded secretaries.

Has Fluidity

"Verbal fluidity" refers to the ability to find the words you need *when you need them*. The more quickly ideas pop into your head, the more readily you can make decisions and solve problems (*and* sound articulate in job interviews!). With practice, you can develop the skill of generating ideas quickly. But if you are tense, it will be much harder to get into the playful frame of mind required for brainstorming and bouncing ideas around.

Exercise:

Practice verbal skills.

There are more than a million words in the English language. Alas, most people depend on the same old few over and over. Further, we don't use those familiar few in novel ways. This exercise is designed to help you to savor the flavor of new verbal entrees.

Can you think of a refreshingly new, non-trite way to express the following?

1. An advertisement for a photographer who takes pictures of children and animals:

   _____

   _____

   _____

2. A description of Margaret Thatcher's strength-coupled-with-femininity:

   _____

   _____

   _____

3. An announcement to keep drinking under control during the holidays:

   _____

   _____

   _____

4. An advertisement for a tennis equipment store:

   _____

   _____

5. An advertisement for a radio talk show of substance, not idle talk:

_____

_____

_____

6. An advertisement for a skilled plumber:

_____

_____

_____

7. A word to suggest that Bill and Hillary Clinton function as a single entity:

_____

_____

_____

8. A judge's exhortation to students participating in a Math Olympics contest:

_____

_____

_____

9. An advertisement for a bank hoping to attract new female customers:

_____

_____

_____

Possible answers. 1. Prints Charming 2. an iron fist inside a velvet glove 3. "Eat, think, and be merry." 4. The Merchant of Tennis 5. Mind over chatter 6. "At your disposal." 7. Billary 8. "May the best math win!" 9. "Girls just wanna have funds."

Exercise:

Stratify.

Stratification is a tool from the world of Total Quality Management (TQM). Teams (and individuals too) use this tool to help discern emerging patterns or trends among seemingly unrelated pieces of information. It can help you to move easily and fluidly among data that may seem disparate at first glance.

Assume that your team has conducted a survey among employees and found that survey participants identified the following as the most common causes of poor morale:

- No one listens
- Meetings don't start on time
- No socializing beyond work
- Projects always take longer than we're led to believe
- Restrooms are never clean
- Teams aren't given the support they need
- Never see the bosses
- Too much pressure, too much stress
- Employees expect managers to have all the answers
- Poor communication
- Managers don't care
- Offices are sterile
- Employees don't care
- Teams aren't given enough direction
- No suggestion program

- We never know what's going on

- Limited cafeteria menu

If you were to stratify or categorize these items, one stratification could easily be Communications. Under it would be listed "No one listens," "Poor communication," "Teams aren't given enough direction," and "We never know what's going on."

What other stratifications would you make and which items would you place in each? (Note: On occasion, an item might fit in more than one stratification.)

Is an Original Thinker

One very tough question job interviewers sometimes use is this: "What was your last original thought?"

How would you answer that one? What is the last totally original idea you had?

Most applicants are thrown off guard by this question. Even after they regain their composure, however, they are still unable to provide an answer. Sensitize yourself to this question and several times a day, ask yourself, "Have I had any totally original thoughts lately?"

Keep a notebook reserved just for recording your original thoughts. Two exercises that encourage original thought are provided on the following pages.

Exercise:

Encourage wild thinking.

Where does wild thinking come from? It's usually sparked by an association that may be quite remote. For example, do you think managers could learn something by studying caterpillars? Read the following, and then see whether you'd answer the same way the second time:

French botanist Henri Fabre discovered something very unusual about "processionary" caterpillars. If he put one down on the ground and lined up a dozen others behind the first, the caterpillars would begin going in a circle—round and round, all of them quite contentedly following the one ahead of them. He wondered what would happen if he put food in the center of the procession. Would any of the caterpillars break out of the circle to get at the food? To his surprise, the caterpillars continued to follow the leader—to their death! Even though salvation was only inches away, not a single one "broke rank" to get at the nourishment.

As you read the Fabre story, you could no doubt draw parallels to the business world. Focus on the secretarial position—of today, of yesterday, of tomorrow—and, as you do, read over the following historical facts. Allow one of them to merge with your thoughts about the secretarial profession. The result should be an original thought.

In 1484, the Portuguese navigator Diego Cam discovered the mouth of the Congo River.

In 1499, Perkin Warbeck tried to escape from the Tower of London.

In 1504, Henry VII placed English guilds/tradesmen under the supervision of the Crown.

In 1507, Orlando Galla of Venice improved the manufacture of glass mirrors.

In 1518, spectacles were created for shortsighted people.

In 1523, the first marine insurance policies were issued in Florence.

In 1539, the first public lottery was held in France.

In 1556, Lutherans were granted equal rights with Catholics via the Peace of Augsburg.

In 1596, Galileo invented the thermometer.

In 1606, an extensive program of road building was begun in France.

In 1612, the last recorded burning of heretics in England occurred.

In 1613, copper coins came into use.

In 1619, William Harvey discovered the circulation of blood.

Some "wild thinking" that might evolve from these historical facts:

1484: Perhaps secretaries need to go on a retreat, as managers do (or at the least, get off-site training), to make plans for the future.

1499: How many secretaries leave (escape) the company each year? A study could be done to compare the cost of raises to the cost of replacements.

1504: Do secretaries need their own union?

1507: What are our mirror images (secretaries in other organizations) doing to improve their lot? Benchmarking could be established.

1518: Are we being shortsighted about our profession? Have we ever spoken to a futurist to learn where our profession is heading?

Explain fully your original thought about secretaries (past, present, or future) based on one of the other historical prompts:

_____

_____

_____

_____

_____

_____

_____

_____

_____

_____

_____

_____

_____

_____

Exercise:

Use models.

A variety of innovation models are helping employees become original thinkers, to improve upon the old and even invent the new. (If you're interested, you can even create models of your own—simply analyze your last several innovations or imaginative contributions and define how you came up with the good idea.) The M3 Model (Moan, Magic, Merge) is a helpful, user-friendly tool. It works like this:

(M1) Moan: What in the current environment is something people are "moaning" about? What is a frequent complaint? A source of annoyance? Some bothersome reality?

(For example, in the pre-computer era, secretaries who needed multiple copies of a document used carbon paper, which was messy and yielded fuzzy copies. Worst of all, though, was the difficulty of correcting mistakes. An eraser or strips of correction tape were used to cover up—not very successfully—the typographical error.)

What is an organizational moan where you work?_____

_____

_____

(M2) Magic: What magic would be needed to solve the organizational moan you identified above? _____

_____

_____

_____

(In the case of your secretarial predecessors, one clever woman thought, "If only I had a little bit of white paint, I could cover up these errors and no one would ever know they were there.")

(M3) Merge: What elements of the magical solution could actually be applied to the workplace? How could you condense, combine, expand, or modify the magical solution to fit your set of circumstances? (The can of white paint, in the previous example, was condensed to a small bottle. And—just as there are different colors of paint, it was not long before there were different colors of "white out.")

Your refined solution: _____

_____

_____

_____

_____

_____

_____

_____

Engages in Metaphorical Thinking

Jose Ortega y Gasset regarded the metaphor as "probably the most fertile power possessed by man." What is this fertile power of the imagination that allows us to bring force and color and imagery to our communications? It is simply a comparison between two things not usually compared.

The metaphor is a tool you can use to capture a far-reaching concept and express it in concrete, easily understood terms. In a study of leaders, Warren Bennis and Burt Nanus found, "A lot of our leaders had a penchant for metaphor, if not for models."

Use a metaphor to translate the complexity of an idea into the simplicity of something practical. Expressing your ideas in metaphoric terms often helps your listeners to grasp a concept more readily. Metaphors are user-friendly, which is why so many leaders employ them. Think of Winston Churchill's reference to the "Iron Curtain," or Jesse Jackson's reference to the "Rainbow Coalition," or Ann Morrison's reference to the "Glass Ceiling." Just as Einstein used the image of a slab of marble to explain a concept in Euclidean geometry, you too can use the net of a metaphor to capture an imagining and bring it into view.

Exercise:

Engage in metaphoric thinking.

A metaphor, as you might remember from your high school English class, is simply a comparison between two things not usually compared.

Look at the following animals and accompanying facts. Select one (or one of your own, if you like) and use it as a metaphor to describe an organizational problem. Then, extend the metaphor to find a solution.

Animal Facts

1. **Elephant** Lives in large family units although the adult male is a solitary creature. Communicates with a "rumbling" in its throat as well as with a loud trumpeting sound. Has soft, padded feet, enabling it to move about almost noiselessly despite its size. Seldom attacks enemies. Travels widely in herds but remains close to water.

2. **Giraffe** Has a unique pattern on its hide—no two "spots" are alike. Flexible front legs allow it to lower its head in order to drink. Elastic blood vessels regulate flow of blood to head, thus preventing loss of consciousness. Can easily camouflage itself. Has very strong skull, which protects it during head-butting. Males neck-wrestle for dominance but seldom hurt each other.

3. Jaguar Remains alone except for breeding season. Is considered an endangered species. Can survive in many different habitats. Does not roar. Known to attack and kill humans, but also just to follow them until they leave its territory.

4. Ape Displays a wide range of emotions with body language. Is social and nurturing. Sleeps in trees at night for protection. Little competition for females. Is skilled at problem solving, recognizes itself in a mirror, suffers human maladies.

The problem-free organization does not exist. Many companies regard problems, in fact, as opportunities for improvement. Specify an organizational problem (opportunity) here— but describe it in metaphoric terms. For example, if you select an alligator, you might say, "Our problem could be compared to an alligator—its danger is masked by its sluggishness. Similarly, our individual and collective inertia is masking a danger. If we do not change, if we do not embrace the new technology, we will soon be trapped—and devoured—in the jaws of obsolescence."

One problem in my organization, depicted metaphorically: _____

_____

_____

A possible solution, depicted metaphorically: _____

_____

_____

_____

Exercise:

Use the metaphor as a springboard.

Jonas Salk, in describing what led him to the polio vaccine, admitted that he learned to think as Mother Nature would think. He asked himself, "How would Nature solve this problem?"

Build your imaginative powers with this exercise. Begin by defining some aspect of your job or the profession as a whole that you feel warrants improvement—the respect that secretaries are accorded, for example, or the pay they earn.

A. What area do you feel needs improvement? _____

_____

_____

_____

_____

B. Now, as you read through the metaphor categories below, list the first five words that come into your mind:

Category	Related Words
• Nature	1. _____
	2. _____
	3. _____
	4. _____
	5. _____

• Sports

1. _____
2. _____
3. _____
4. _____
5. _____

• Cooking

1. _____
2. _____
3. _____
4. _____
5. _____

• Entertainment

1. _____
2. _____
3. _____
4. _____
5. _____

C. Now select one of the categories in Part B and think within it. Try to solve the problem you described in Part A in terms of one of the words you've listed for the category. If the solution is not coming to you, select another person or thing or even another category. Continue doing this (perhaps even making up categories of your own) until you come across an idea you think will work.

Use this formula: "If I think as (<u>insert word from a category</u>) would think, one possible solution to the problem of (<u>insert problem from Part A</u>) would be (<u>your solution</u>)."

Now you try it:

If I think as _____ would think, one possible solution

to the problem of _____

_____

would be _____

_____

_____

_____

_____

_____

_____

Is Willing to Look Beyond the Surface

Nobel Prize-winning biochemist Albert Szent-Gyorgyi asserted that "discovery consists of looking at the same thing as everyone else and thinking something different."

The former secretary to Supreme Court Justice Ruth Bader Ginsburg looked at the same thing her boss looked at and yet saw something else. Justice Bader acknowledges her debt to her secretary for her switch from the term "sex discrimination" to the more equitable "gender discrimination": "I owe it all to my secretary at Columbia Law School, who said, 'I'm typing all these briefs and articles for you and the word "sex," "sex," "sex" is on every page. Don't you know that those nine men (on the Supreme Court)—they hear that word, and their first association is not the way you want them to be thinking? Why don't you use the word "gender"? It is a grammatical term, and it will ward off distracting associations.' "

Innovation is preceded by a willingness to change and make changes. It is also preceded by the ability to "look at the same thing as everyone else," and yet to think something different. This power of the imagination, in the words of Bernadine Waters and Teiana McPike, support staff personnel from Johnson Controls, Inc., makes us "capable of reaching beyond existing reality."

If Jonas Salk viewed himself as both a scientist and naturalist, ask yourself what else you are—in addition to being a secretary. This extension beyond the literal will help you broaden the scope of your thinking.

Exercise:

Accept input from anywhere.

Are you blocking your own creative potential? Answer the following questions to find out. Be as honest as possible—the survey won't provide any insight unless you approach it with an open attitude. If you cover up the truth, you can't uncover the barriers blocking your imaginative capacity.

Answer each question on the basis of   1 = Never;   2 = Seldom;   3 = Often;   4 = Always.

1. ___ I am stimulated by complex problems.

2. ___ I experiment with unusual combinations.

3. ___ My colleagues think of me as a source of innovative ideas.

4. ___ I read voraciously, both in and outside my field.

5. ___ I associate with people who have decidedly different viewpoints or orientations.

6. ___ I search for better ways of doing things.

7. ___ I am asked for my opinion on tough-to-solve situations.

8. ___ I entertain new ideas with enthusiasm rather than cynicism.

9. ___ I scold myself for thinking absurd thoughts.

10. ___ I make decisions after considering a number of possibilities.

11. ___ I ask a lot of questions.

12. ___ I worry about appearing foolish.

13. ___ I enjoy learning new things.

14. ___ I encourage open discussion.

15. ___   I believe disagreeing can be healthy.

16. ___   I like to have my thinking challenged.

17. ___   I believe logic can solve every problem.

18. ___   I am impatient with rigid problem-solvers.

19. ___   I am mentally playful.

20. ___   I follow rules and recipes to the letter.

21. ___   I daydream.

22. ___   I like/understand expressions such as "Architecture is frozen music."

23. ___   I can see why Peter Drucker advised a would-be executive to learn to play the violin.

24. ___   I engage in what Einstein termed "wildly speculative thinking."

25. ___   I synthesize pieces of knowledge into new entities.

A "perfect" score for the perfect innovator would be 88—four points for every question except #9, #12, #17, and #20 (each of which would earn only one point). However, as there are no perfect people, think of your score as being on a continuum. No matter where you placed, pledge to acquire more of the innovator's traits by engaging in some of the behaviors suggested here—allowing yourself more daydreaming time, for example.

Exercise:

Make work fun.

A number of management gurus—Tom Peters, W. Edwards Deming, Michael LeBoeuf—assert that work should be fun, that if we enjoy what we do, we'll do it better. Perhaps in support of this tenet or perhaps because the opposite of fun (excessive stress) can diminish productivity, a number of organizations are forming "joy gangs." A joy gang is a team that meets regularly to discover ways to make the workplace a more enjoyable place to be. On the surface, it may seem that work is not supposed to be fun, but the truth is we are willing to work harder when we take pleasure in our work place and our work mates.

Assume that the leader of your joy gang has asked you and the other members of the team to prepare a list of fifteen ways to bring joy to the workplace. What would you put on your list?

1. _____
2. _____
3. _____
4. _____
5. _____
6. _____
7. _____
8. _____
9. _____
10. _____
11. _____

12. _____

13. _____

14. _____

15. _____

Which of the ideas on your list are you most likely to attempt to implement? _____

_____

_____

_____

_____

What might keep you from implementing them? _____

_____

_____

_____

_____

_____

Has the Courage Not to Conform

There is an undeniable security in knowing that we don't stand alone. And yet, avant-garde thinkers and innovators have always had to stand on their own, at least at some point. The average follower will not leave the fold, or the old, until the fold itself is embracing the new. Before that happens, however, the leader remains a lone voice, a visionary who must suffer the "slings and arrows" of nonacceptance.

It takes courage to step outside existing boundaries. It requires self-confidence to stand by your plan and await the endorsement of others.

Exercise:

Use your multiple facets.

Innovative secretaries know they are much more, and can be much more, than the label of their job titles. There is more they can do if they choose not to conform to their standard responsibilities. Even if you don't have the power to change your official designation, you might create an unofficial designation. Consider what one secretary in Flagstaff, Arizona, did: she proclaimed herself "Czarina of the Coffee Room." Since she was responsible for collecting money for and purchasing coffee supplies, she decided to turn her supplemental responsibility into a sphere of influence. She began signing her memos (regarding the coffee collections) and notices in the coffee room with her new title. In her own creative way, she brought levity into the lives of many people and reduced somewhat the onerous aspects of being in charge of coffee.

Here is a list of "personas" that members of effective support staff teams use to describe themselves. The list was compiled by support staff personnel from Johnson Controls, Inc.: Sandy Hagemann, Jenn Lisser, Patty Kachelski, Dawn Tietyen, Sue Wisnewski, Carol Ryan, Barbara Nenorth, Carol Matter, Bonnie Lenz, Eileen Burkman, and Cathy McCash.

Leader	Facilitator
Devil's advocate	Timekeeper
Minister	Delegator
Surgeon	Peacekeeper
Analyzer	Nominator
Instigator	Genius
Scribe	Problem solver
Idealist	Cheerleader

Babysitter	Presenter
Confidence builder	Designer
Seller	Marketer
Dreamer	Authority figure

You are, we all are, many different people rolled into one unique entity. Unfortunately, many of us ignore the possibilities lying within us; we fail to break down boundaries and probe the personas we are and can be.

What additional roles do you play as you perform your job?

_____

_____

_____

_____

_____

Which personas are you best at? _____

_____

_____

Which do you most need to improve? _____

_____

_____

Exercise:

Form alliances.

The opportunities to form partnerships exist all around you—intraorganizationally, interorganizationally, intranationally, and even internationally. Did you know, for example, about the International Symposium of Secretaries? The president of the Brazilian National Federation of Secretaries, Leida Maria de Moraes, shared results of the First International Symposium with attendees at the 1994 Professional Secretaries International® Convention (held in Orlando, Florida). These are their proposals:

1. ***To continue holding an International Symposium for Secretaries.*** Conchita Delgado, CPS, was asked to write to secretarial associations around the world to determine criteria for holding the symposium (including frequency) and for selecting the host country. Conchita has already mailed a questionnaire and is waiting for the responses.

2. ***To create an International Code of Ethics for the profession.*** This area is being coordinated by Elisa del Pino, from Spain, assisted by Isabel Cirilo, from Portugal. The code would contain guidelines for professional secretaries in the different countries regarding their behavior in the working world.

3. ***To designate an International Secretaries Day.*** This is being coordinated by Sheila Avakin, from Uruguay, assisted by Carmina Gutierrez, from Bolivia. November 30 was selected as the date since this was the date on which the First International Symposium for Secretaries began. This observance would be in addition to the individual dates in which countries observe Secretaries Day.

4. ***To create a worldwide organization for secretaries.*** This area is being coordinated by Leida Maria de Moraes, representing Brazil. Countries are being invited to submit suggestions on criteria for

goals, functions, and so forth for the establishment of the organization.

5. *To declare the International Year of the Secretary.* This is being coordinated by Inocencia Barreto, from Paraguay, assisted by Elvira de Enciso, from Peru. In this case, it would be necessary to contact the United Nations.

Ms. Moraes concluded her remarks with a quotation from Pierre Teilhard de Chardin, the French philosopher:

> "Truthfully I doubt that there may be a more decisive minute for a thinking being than that in which—realizing the truth—he discovers that he is not a lost element in the cosmic solitude, but a universal determination to live that converges and humanizes in him."

If you would like to be a part of the universal determination being shared by secretaries around the world, you may contact Leida Maria de Moraes at the Federacao Nacional das Secretarias:

Rua Aimberê, 2064

Sumaré

01258-020

São Paulo SP Brazil

By joining an international secretarial organization or by doing any other activity that goes beyond your job description, you will be showing your ability not to conform to narrow definitions—definitions that were probably established by someone in your organization a long time ago and that haven't been updated since. To be sure, there are organizational policies to which you must conform. But there's also a whole world of growth opportunities that do not conform to the limited descriptions that have been established for secretarial behaviors. Explore your capabilities. Explore your world.

INTERVIEW: Administrative Support/Secretarial Enrichment Team (ASSET), Mount Carmel Health Center, Columbus, Ohio.

Mount Carmel Health includes Mount Carmel Medical Center, a 462-bed tertiary care teaching hospital; Mount Carmel East Hospital, a 287-bed community hospital; and the Community Services Corporation, which oversees Hospice, Community Outreach, and Home Care. Mount Carmel Health also operates a Graduate Medical Education Program, a College of Nursing, and a Preferred Provider Organization. Mount Carmel Health is a member of the Holy Cross Health System, a nationwide non-profit organization sponsored by the Sisters of the Holy Cross, South Bend, Indiana.

Q: *How did ASSET evolve?*

A: Ten years ago, a very small group of secretaries met to plan a first annual seminar to celebrate Professional Secretaries Day at Mount Carmel Health. This group also tried to have monthly meetings, but these were met with little enthusiasm or attendance by secretaries at the hospital until five years ago.

At that time, some new secretaries joined the planning team and the group met to discuss the challenges of the future. We asked ourselves several questions: Were we going to eliminate monthly meetings and only plan an annual seminar? If we were going to continue monthly meetings, how could we get our group recognized and increase attendance at the meetings? Were there things we could do to improve our workplace? As a result of this brainstorming session, we made several decisions:

1. We decided to cut back to quarterly meetings, one of which would be the annual seminar.

2. Our group needed a name that would be recognized by secretaries, other support personnel, and their supervisors.

   Because the group had been called by several different names over the years, we felt that the people we were trying to reach didn't always realize that the meetings we scheduled applied to them. Our goal was to reach all secretaries and other administrative support personnel such as unit secretaries, which involves approximately 300-plus associates at Mount Carmel Health. We chose the name "ASSET," which reflected our desire to be an asset to the hospital.

   We designed our logo to represent the hands of the workers supporting the hospital. We then used this logo in our announcements of meetings and purchased tote bags imprinted with the logo as a gift for those who attended the next seminar. We continue to use this logo on all of our mailings and our gifts each year.

3. We needed a mission statement to define our goals. It was enthusiastically approved by Administration.

4. We needed to seek support and guidance from Hospital Administration.

Q: *How did ASSET obtain support from Administration?*

A: We invited the Director of Human Resources to meet with us. (We bribed him with lunch!) We explained our goals and hopes for the future and asked for his support. At the end of our presentation, he admitted to us that he came to our meeting with trepidation, fearing that it was going to be a gripe session, not a group seeking ways to contribute to the quality of the workplace! He was very enthusiastic about our ideas and asked to be part of our group. He offered to speak to the Executive Vice President about our group and helped us schedule a meeting with her. This was done and she too became an enthusiastic "cheerleader" for ASSET.

We asked for and received permission to address a management meeting. We asked for management's support and encouragement for their secretaries and other support personnel to attend our meetings.

Q: *What is your mission statement?*

A: It reads, "Dedicated to the spirit of Mount Carmel Health, ASSET exists to enrich the professional life of administrative support/secretarial associates by:

- Improving interdepartmental and intradepartmental communications;
- Facilitating problem solving and improving morale;

- Establishing a modem of support in order to help each other achieve:

    a) personal and professional growth

    b) better performance

    c) job satisfaction

    d) motivation and enthusiasm

- Recognizing and affirming one another's achievement;

- Conducting open meetings that will be flexible, with all members having an equal voice;

- Promoting educational endeavors;

- Seeking to understand, and then to be understood."

 What organizational innovations is ASSET involved with?

A: We are preparing a concise resource manual for all departments. We think this will be of the most benefit to secretaries but will also be a valuable tool for managers. This resource manual will explain how to use forms such as check requests, petty cash vouchers, and expense request forms; how to make travel plans; how to request services from various hospital departments; how to reserve a conference room; and many other issues common to all departments.

Our committee is asking to be notified by Human Resources whenever a new secretary or other clerical person is hired so that we can introduce ourselves to them, extend a personal invitation to our meetings, and most of all, act as a mentor to help guide the new associate—especially during his or her early weeks at the hospital.

We are also planning to publish a quarterly newsletter, to be mailed one month prior to each quarterly meeting.

We prepared guidelines for file retention and distributed them to all department managers and secretaries. Our entire organization now has a File Clean Out Day every July.

We are looking at creating task forces to address projects suggested at our recent annual seminar. We received many ideas we think we can implement.

The Planning Committee was invited to establish standards and to select desk chairs for use across the organization.

The Planning Committee has been invited to participate on other task forces and committees, including e-mail program selection and the Performance Improvement Committee.

The Planning Committee was awarded the first Team SPIRIT Award and received special pins and certificates (awarded to them at a Joint Management Meeting with 300 people present).

 How does the Administration view ASSET?

This quote from Jo-Ann Burke, the executive vice president for Mount Carmel Health, best reflects our partnership: "We on the senior management level appreciate and endorse ASSET's efforts."

Conclusion

We are living in times of tremendous turmoil, tremendous change. And the pace of change will continue at astonishing levels. When you consider that more information was produced in the time span between 1965 and 1995 than between 3000 B.C. and 1965, then you begin to get a sense of the intellectual upheaval in which we are participating. Imagination is driving those changes—and in this information era, the most valuable employees will be those who continuously acquire information and apply it to produce innovative solutions.

The information contained in the preceding pages was presented to share with you traits of imaginative individuals, believing that creativity, like most other traits, can be developed. The exercises associated with each trait offer practice in refining your existing skills and exploring those you haven't yet acquired. Sharpening those creative skills will lead to the vision needed for innovation. That vision, however, needs nurturing—nurturing to develop the art of imagining. As Jonathan Swift declared, "Vision is the art of seeing things invisible."

Can you answer "yes" to at least one of these questions?

- Do you view chaos as a possible source of dynamic thought?

- Do you seek information from multiple sources?

- Are you willing to try new things?

- Have you experienced the "magic of thinking big"?

If you can, then you have learned your lessons well. Know that others, wondrously successful others, are also answering "yes" to the same questions. (Witness the "BHAGs" established by Wal-Mart founder, Sam Walton. These "Big Hairy Audacious Goals" drove him to make his first store the most profitable one in the whole state within a five-year period). You should be ready now to set some BHAGs of your own.

Those BHAGs will lead to having greater visibility focused on your competencies. Accept the challenges and be guided by your confidence—in yourself, in your ideas, in your team, and in your ability to make a difference.

Secretaries hold a pivotal place in the organizational hierarchy. As they assume responsibilities more managerial in nature, so will they assume higher levels of empowerment and recompense. Because the traditional "command-and-control" style of management is being discarded in many places, solutions to problems are welcomed from all levels of the organization. With a growing increase of "open-book" management thinking, secretaries are privy to more knowledge than ever before. And knowledge, of course, is power.

The time is ripe for the innovative secretary to seize that power and seize the moment too. With innovative thinking, a secretary can alter the course of his or her own destiny and the course of the profession as well.

Bibliography
and Suggested
Reading

Adams, James L. *Conceptual Blockbusting: A Guide to Better Ideas.*
Reading, MA: Addison-Wesley, 1986.

Albrecht, Karl. *Brain Power: Learn to Improve Your Thinking Skills.*
Englewood Cliffs, NJ: Prentice-Hall, 1980.

Briggs, John. *Fire in the Crucible: The Alchemy of Creative Genius.* New
York: St. Martin's Press, 1988.

Buzan, Tony. *Use Both Sides of Your Brain.* New York: E.P. Dutton,
1983.

Csikszentmihalyi, Mihaly. *Flow: The Psychology of Optimal Experience.*
New York: Harper & Row, 1990.

Fixx, James. *Solve It: A Perplexing Profusion of Puzzles.* Garden City,
NY: Doubleday, 1978.

Foster, Richard N. *Innovation: An Attacker's Advantage.* New York:
Summit Books, 1986.

Rico, Gabrielle Lusser. *Writing the Natural Way: Using Right-Brain
Techniques to Release Your Expressive Powers.* Los Angeles: J.P.
Tarcher, 1983.

Ruggiero, Vincent. *The Art of Thinking: A Guide to Critical and Creative Thought*. New York: Harper & Row, 1984.

Senge, Peter M. *The Fifth Discipline: The Art and Practice of the Learning Organization*. New York: Doubleday Currency, 1990.

Thompson, Charles. *What a Great Idea: The Key Steps Creative People Take*. New York: HarperPerennial, 1992.

von Oech, Roger. *A Kick in the Seat of the Pants: Using Your Explorer, Artist, Judge, and Warrior to Be More Creative*. New York: Harper & Row, 1986.

Yusuda, Yuzo. *40 Years, 20 Million Suggestions: The Toyota Suggestion System*. Cambridge, MA: Productivity Press, 1991.

Available From
SkillPath Publications

Self-Study Sourcebooks

Climbing the Corporate Ladder: What You Need to Know and Do to Be a Promotable Person *by Barbara Pachter and Marjorie Brody*

Coping With Supervisory Nightmares: 12 Common Nightmares of Leadership and What You Can Do About Them *by Michael and Deborah Singer Dobson*

Defeating Procrastination: 52 Fail-Safe Tips for Keeping Time on Your Side *by Marlene Caroselli, Ed.D.*

Discovering Your Purpose *by Ivy Haley*

Going for the Gold: Winning the Gold Medal for Financial Independence *by Lesley D. Bissett, CFP*

Having Something to Say When You Have to Say Something: The Art of Organizing Your Presentation *by Randy Horn*

Info-Flood: How to Swim in a Sea of Information Without Going Under *by Marlene Caroselli, Ed.D.*

The Innovative Secretary *by Marlene Caroselli, Ed.D.*

Letters & Memos: Just Like That! *by Dave Davies*

Mastering the Art of Communication: Your Keys to Developing a More Effective Personal Style *by Michelle Fairfield Poley*

Organized for Success! 95 Tips for Taking Control of Your Time, Your Space, and Your Life *by Nanci McGraw*

A Passion to Lead! How to Develop Your Natural Leadership Ability *by Michael Plumstead*

P.E.R.S.U.A.D.E.: Communication Strategies That Move People to Action *by Marlene Caroselli, Ed.D.*

Productivity Power: 250 Great Ideas for Being More Productive *by Jim Temme*

Promoting Yourself: 50 Ways to Increase Your Prestige, Power, and Paycheck *by Marlene Caroselli, Ed.D.*

Proof Positive: How to Find Errors Before They Embarrass You *by Karen L. Anderson*

Risk-Taking: 50 Ways to Turn Risks Into Rewards *by Marlene Caroselli, Ed.D. and David Harris*

Speak Up and Stand Out: How to Make Effective Presentations *by Nanci McGraw*

Stress Control: How You Can Find Relief From Life's Daily Stress *by Steve Bell*

The Technical Writer's Guide *by Robert McGraw*

Total Quality Customer Service: How to Make It Your Way of Life *by Jim Temme*

Write It Right! A Guide for Clear and Correct Writing *by Richard Andersen and Helene Hinis*

Your Total Communication Image *by Janet Signe Olson, Ph.D.*

Handbooks

The ABC's of Empowered Teams: Building Blocks for Success *by Mark Towers*

Assert Yourself! Developing Power-Packed Communication Skills to Make Your Points Clearly, Confidently, and Persuasively *by Lisa Contini*

Breaking the Ice: How to Improve Your On-the-Spot Communication Skills *by Deborah Shouse*

The Care and Keeping of Customers: A Treasury of Facts, Tips, and Proven Techniques for Keeping Your Customers Coming BACK! *by Roy Lantz*

Challenging Change: Five Steps for Dealing With Change *by Holly DeForest and Mary Steinberg*

Dynamic Delegation: A Manager's Guide for Active Empowerment *by Mark Towers*

Every Woman's Guide to Career Success *by Denise M. Dudley*

Grammar? No Problem! *by Dave Davies*

Great Openings and Closings: 28 Ways to Launch and Land Your Presentations With Punch, Power, and Pizazz *by Mari Pat Varga*

Hiring and Firing: What Every Manager Needs to Know *by Marlene Caroselli, Ed.D. with Laura Wyeth, Ms.Ed.*

How to Be a More Effective Group Communicator: Finding Your Role and Boosting Your Confidence in Group Situations *by Deborah Shouse*

How to Deal With Difficult People *by Paul Friedman*

Learning to Laugh at Work: The Power of Humor in the Workplace *by Robert McGraw*

Making Your Mark: How to Develop a Personal Marketing Plan for Becoming More Visible and More Appreciated at Work *by Deborah Shouse*

Meetings That Work *by Marlene Caroselli, Ed.D.*

The Mentoring Advantage: How to Help Your Career Soar to New Heights *by Pam Grout*

Minding Your Business Manners: Etiquette Tips for Presenting Yourself Professionally in Every Business Situation *by Marjorie Brody and Barbara Pachter*

Misspeller's Guide *by Joel and Ruth Schroeder*

Motivation in the Workplace: How to Motivate Workers to Peak Performance and Productivity *by Barbara Fielder*

NameTags Plus: Games You Can Play When People Don't Know What to Say *by Deborah Shouse*

Networking: How to Creatively Tap Your People Resources *by Colleen Clarke*

New & Improved! 25 Ways to Be More Creative and More Effective *by Pam Grout*

Power Write! A Practical Guide to Words That Work *by Helene Hinis*

The Power of Positivity: Eighty ways to energize your life *by Joel and Ruth Schroeder*

Putting Anger to Work For You *by Ruth and Joel Schroeder*

Reinventing Your Self: 28 Strategies for Coping With Change *by Mark Towers*

Saying "No" to Negativity: How to Manage Negativity in Yourself, Your Boss, and Your Co-Workers *by Zoie Kaye*

The Supervisor's Guide: The Everyday Guide to Coordinating People and Tasks *by Jerry Brown and Denise Dudley, Ph.D.*

Taking Charge: A Personal Guide to Managing Projects and Priorities *by Michal E. Feder*

Treasure Hunt: 10 Stepping Stones to a New and More Confident You! *by Pam Grout*

A Winning Attitude: How to Develop Your Most Important Asset! *by Michelle Fairfield Poley*

For more information, call 1-800-873-7545.

Notes

Notes